# THAMESIDE MOLESEY

FRONT COVER: Molesey Lock and Rollers, c1905.

Peaceful Molesey – beloved by many artists: a 19th century study, initialled J.H. and entitled 'Moulsey'.

# THAMESIDE MOLESEY

A towpath ramble from
Hampton Court to Hampton Reach

ROWLAND G.M. BAKER
and
GWENDOLINE F. BAKER

BARON
Buckingham
MMVII

Originally published in 1989
Second impression 1990
Third impression 2007

**PUBLISHED BY BARON BOOKS OF BUCKINGHAM
IN THIS THIRD IMPRESSION
PRODUCED BY THE BATH PRESS AND
ACADEMIC + TECHNICAL TYPESETTING**

© Gwendoline F. Baker

All rights reserved. No part of this publication may be reproduced, stored in a retrieval system, or transmitted, in any form or by any means, electronic, mechanical, photocopying, recording or otherwise, without the prior permission of Baron Books.

Any copy of this book issued by the Publisher as clothbound or as a paperback is sold subject to the condition that it shall not by way of trade or otherwise, be lent, re-sold, hired out or otherwise circulated without the Publisher's prior consent, in any form of binding or condition including this condition being imposed on a subsequent purchaser.

ISBN 0 86023 414 2

# Contents

| | |
|---|---|
| Foreword by Derek Brown | 8 |
| Acknowledgements | 9 |
| Introduction | 9 |
| Liquid History | 10 |
| Cigarette Island | 15 |
| Hampton Court Bridge | 20 |
| Thames Taverns | 32 |
| Lock and Weir | 37 |
| Floods, Fields and Fines | 51 |
| Molesey Boat Club | 57 |
| Tagg's Island | 65 |
| Fred Westcott | 79 |
| Karsino | 83 |
| Willow'd Aytes | 95 |
| Garrick's Villa | 102 |
| The Bathing Station | 107 |
| The Hurst: Cradle of Cricket | 108 |
| A Bloody Rendez-Vous | 113 |
| Hampton Races | 117 |
| Hurst Park | 122 |
| Hampton Reach | 132 |
| Bibliography | 137 |
| Index | 138 |
| Subscribers | 140 |

# FOREWORD *by Derek Brown*

This is Rowland Baker's last book and there could be no more fitting swansong. He was born in Molesey and as a child he wandered all round the district, exploring every road and path. The towpath beside the Thames was a great attraction and he was always stirred when walking among such scenes of gentle beauty.

He decided at a young age to collect everything that he could relating to Molesey's past, with an ambition eventually to write the history of his native place. *The Book of Molesey*, published a year before his death, is the splendid memorial of him and his life's work.

The opening of the present Molesey Library was a great pleasure: he saw it as the final repository for his extensive collection. He arranged an exhibition under the title of Joseph Palmer's poem, 'Dear peaceful Molesey, ever in my mind' showing a wealth of riverside pictures and photographs.

Molesey, its rivers and walks, were ever in his mind, so that his friends, reading this book, will keep him in mind and hear his voice again and recall his smiling enthusiasm as they ramble with him in spirit along the towpath. Readers who own this book will share his quiet enjoyment.

### *NOTE TO THIRD IMPRESSION*
This impression has been published by kind permission of the author's widow, Mrs Gwen Baker, and with the assistance of her son, Steve Baker, and made possible by the Molesey Residents Association and its members.

# DEDICATION

To Martin and Steven

# Acknowledgements

The authors are indebted to the people of Molesey who have told of their lives, shown or lent their pictures and records and allowed us into their homes. They are too many to mention by name, and sadly some are not now with us. Most will recognise themselves and remember their contributions, and we hope they will take this as our gratitude for their help and support. Once again, we must stress that anyone who ventures into local history must be grateful for the help given by public libraries and record offices. From national collections down to local ones, librarians and archivists seem always helpful, willing and courteous. We would like particularly to mention Molesey Library, Thames Ditton Library, Kingston Heritage Centre, Surrey Records Office, Surrey Local Record Office, British Library and Colindale Newspaper Library, Trustees of the British Museum, Hunting Aerofilms Ltd, Aerial Photography, and to thank most sincerely the staff of each and all of them.

Once again we are grateful to the Clerk of the old Esher UDC for allowing access to books and papers within his care and to Mrs Sally Ward for typing the manuscript.

Finally our thanks go to Mr Clive Birch of Barracuda Books, and to Mr Derek Brown, for kindly writing the foreword to this book.

# Introduction

How one can best classify this little volume is difficult to say. It is not intended that it should be yet another Thames guide book, (there are so many, which cover a much wider area than this book hopes to do). Neither is it entirely a chapter out of the district's long and fascinating past, nor an anthology of river literature, not yet just a retrospect of the author's personal riverside memories. Nevertheless it somehow contrives to be a confusion of all of these – local history – anthology – nostalgia, a *vade-mecum* for all would be ramblers of the towpath.

The author has known the riverside for well over half a century. The Thames has been a place in which to swim, on which to boat, and alongside which to stroll. In wartime it was something to be guarded, in peace it was somewhere to court. It has been a pleasurable experience he would share with others, by leading the reader on a ramble along the towpath of Molesey's river. For, like John Taylor, the seventeenth century water poet, he declares:

'Noble Thames, whilst I can hold a pen,
I will divulge thy glory unto men'.

*Note:* Sadly the author died after completing the text for this, his second book on Molesey's past; his widow, Gwen, has searched out the illustrations and their captions from her husband's records, adding her own affectionate knowledge of the same riverside, and her own, independent researches. Obviously some inevitable recent changes may have taken place since the text was completed in 1987.

ABOVE: The Molesey Thames in 1907 – seen from the Surrey bank, with the houseboat *Gypsy* above and below, Hampton Church and Garrick House. BELOW: The journey starts, on the towpath at Molesey, early this century.

# LIQUID HISTORY

In comparison with some of the massive waterways in other parts of the world, the Thames is merely an insignificant stream. There are no towering gorges, no magnificent waterfalls, no rapid cataracts.

'But none in charm surpasses England's own,
Thames or Isis, river known to song'.

In length, in breadth, and in nobility it is far surpassed by many others. 'But', as John Burns said, in an oft-quoted retort when chided on this score by some transatlantic visitors, 'every drop of the River Thames is liquid 'istory'. And surely there can be few parts of the river, outside the capital itself, to which this maxim can apply with greater justification than the three miles or so between Hampton Court and Sunbury Lock, where it forms the northern boundary of East and West Molesey. Murray's *Guide to Surrey* (1898) says: 'The walk along the towing-path on the left bank from Hampton Court to Walton Bridge is one to be recommended'. It was so then – it is so now.

Although the scenery here is perhaps not a prospect of breathtaking grandeur, nevertheless neither is it a tedium of monotony and boredom. Almost every step opens up a view of something different – an island, a building, some river craft. Each has its own story, its own characteristic associations with the history, customs or literature of England. It is rather like the girl next door, the girl who is not a ravishing beauty, but who has, however, the sort of pretty face and graceful figure with which one falls in love.

Samuel Carter Hall and his wife Anna Maria, Victorian writers, who at one time lived in Palace Road, wrote in *The Book of the Thames* (1869) 'The Thames is the King of Island Rivers; if deficient in the grander features of landscape, it is rich in pictorial beauty; its associations are closely linked with heroic men and glorious achievements, its antiquities are of the rarest and most instructive order; its natural productions of the highest interest; it wanders through fertile meads and beside pleasant banks, gathering strength from a thousand tributaries; on either side are remains of ancient grandeur, homely villages, retired cottages, palatial dwellings, and populous cities and towns; boats and barges, and sea-craft of a hundred nations, indicate and enhance its wealth; numerous locks and bridges facilitate its navigation and promote the traffic that gives it fame. Its history is that of England'.

Soulless indeed must he be who is not moved by the riverscape's natural charm, its subtlety and variety, its moods and caprices, whether it be viewed *'en fete'* for a sunny summer's regatta, or festooned with the icy rime of winter, during the soft breeze of morning, or when the setting sun drenches the silent water with a rose-red hue.

One may find however, that the best time to ramble the towpath is when timely spring's green leaves and pink blossom line the waterside, or on one of those fine sunny days that often occur in October or early November, when autumn sets its golden-brown on the trees and turns the creeper to russet-red. Then one may saunter and have the riverside almost to oneself without the tourist crowds to disconcert one's thoughts. Then might the mind shuttle back and forth from present to past, conjuring pictures of incidents, fifty, a hundred, even a thousand or more years ago, back to the time when the river was worn and shaped, gouged out of the ground by a receding glacier at the end of some ante-historical ice-age. How many feet, one may ponder, have trod this self-same path since our primeval ancestors paddled their dug-out log canoes through the lonesome river, leaving their craft to be found in its muddy bed centuries later.

Historical retrospectives are not all that will crowd the rambler's mind. The riverside is rich in literary and artistic associations; poets and authors, painters and actors, have crowded to its banks. Countless pens have waxed lyrical of its captivating charm since Edmund Spenser, over four hundred years ago, wrote in *Prothalamion* (1596):

> 'Along the shoars of silver streaming Thames;
> Whose rutty bank, the which his river hems,
> Was painted all with variable flowers,
> And all the meads adorned with dainty gems,
> Fit to deck maidens bowers, and crown their paramours
> Against the bridal day, which is not long;
> Sweet Thames! run softly, till I end my song'.

Our particular stretch of the river has been beloved by many artists and photographers. The most notable was probably Alfred Sisley, the French Impressionist, who spent almost a whole year here in 1874, usually with his easel set up somewhere along the towpath. He loved rivers, and the Thames around Molesey reminded him of his precious Seine. The results are now scattered in art galleries and private collections around the world. They depict the river through its many facets – the gaily garlanded regatta, the lock, the water thundering over the weir, the crowded towpath, the bridge – a unique record of Molesey's riverside as it existed over a century ago.

The very name 'Thames' is ancient. We find it mentioned by Julius Caesar half a century before Christ. It derives from a British word meaning 'dark' – the dark river, and appears analogous to the Sanskrit *'Tamasa'*, the name of a tributary of the Ganges. In the middle ages it was variously spelled: Temese, Temesa, Tamise, Temmes, and Tems.

West Molesey towpath, where bathers dawdle, a panama-hatted fisherman sits motionless in the reeds, and the yachts go sailing by.

ABOVE: The towpath above the Lock at Molesey in 1910 was just the place to parade in your Sunday best.

CENTRE: Hampton Court Station – point of departure.

BELOW: The *Duke of York* steamer at the Lock.

13

ABOVE: The Castle Inn, Tagg's Thames Hotel and the third Hampton Court Bridge – plus the small bridge over the creek (centre background). BELOW: Alfred Sisley painted Molesey Lock in 1874.

# CIGARETTE ISLAND

Perhaps the best point from which to start our ramble is Hampton Court station. Indeed, it has been so for thousands since the railway first came here in 1849, and brought the riverside within a cheap day's excursion for urban dwellers in all parts of the metropolis.

The station stands on what was before 1930, an island. At that time the River Mole flowed prettily along the side of Creek Road, whence it bubbled out from under the wheels of East Molesey Mill – and entered the Thames approximately where the present bridge now stands.

This part of the Mole was known locally as 'The Creek' – hence Creek Road. Access to the station was by means of two rickety wooden bridges, one for pedestrians and one for vehicles which, as the author remembers as a young boy, shook violently whenever one of the horse-drawn cabs, which used to ply from the station, crossed over.

James Thorne, who rambled the River Mole in 1844, describing the scene, says: 'The termination of the Mole is a noble one. From its mouth the Thames, with Hampton Court on the opposite bank, form a picture of surpassing beauty'. This surpassing beauty attracted many artists. Sir James Thornhill, who painted the ceilings in the palace across the water, captured the view in a pen and ink sketch in 1731, which is now displayed in the Whitworth Art Gallery in Manchester. The British Museum has a delightful little water-colour from exactly the same spot, executed by Girtin in 1800.

The seventeenth century pastoral poet, Michael Drayton, in a long epic about the English countryside, allegorises the Thames as the son of Thame and Isis, a princely youth, who sets out to find a bride and on the journey: 'Gainst Hampton Court he meets the soft and gentle Mole.' *Poly-Olbion* (1622). He tarries here and woos this fair maiden, but his parents disapproved of the alliance, wishing him instead to court the beautiful Medway. He eventually allows himself to be persuaded, but is so loth to leave his adored Mole that twice a day: 'Up towards the place, where first his much-loved Mole was seen, He ever since doth flow beyond delightful Shene'. It must be remembered that, in Drayton's time, before Teddington Lock was constructed, the tide flowed up to, and even beyond, this spot.

John Stapleton sees the scene somewhat differently, as the rather somnambulent Mole suddenly rouses to find itself mingling with the waters of the larger river:

'Now lo! the Mole, awakening from a dream,
Seeks for absorption in the Thames's stream'. (1878)

In the early 1930s, when Hampton Court Way was constructed, to form an approach to the new bridge, the Mole was diverted into the River Ember above East Molesey Mill and the Creek was filled in.

The ancient name of Cigarette Island was 'The Sterte', mentioned as early as 1306, and which almost certainly comes from the Old English word '*Steart*', a tail of land, an apt description of its situation between the two rivers. In 1843 it was called 'Davis's Ait', after the family of Davis who at one time kept the nearby Castle Inn. The present name derives from a houseboat called *Cigarette* which used to be moored here. Now, no longer a true island, the name is applied to the five acres of public open space behind the station.

Much of this land was at one time used for the growing of osiers or withies, which were collected, peeled, dried, and sold for the manufacture of baskets.

The reach on the Surrey side was lined with a row of houseboats, all gaily painted, elaborately ornamented and flower bedecked, a truly brilliant scene. The *Cigarette* belonged to Sir Henry Foreman, Member of Parliament and Mayor of Hammersmith. Besides this there was *Wildflower*, a massive 110 feet in length – almost half as much again as *Cigarette* and others with names like *Mimosa, Castle, Nirvana, Happy Days* and *Cheznous*. To own a houseboat was a fashionable thing. The surroundings were arcadian, yet within easy reach of town. The decks were usually resplendent with cheerful awnings, girls in pretty summer frocks and men in flannels and boaters.

Houseboats were particularly popular with music hall artists and with the gay young set of the times. Sometimes the peace of a summer's evening might be disturbed by the sound of a wild Bohemian party. Among those supposed to have owned houseboats off Cigarette Island at some time are Harry Tate, Marie Lloyd, Charles Austin, the McNaughton Brothers, Fred Kitchin and Lord Egmont, all household names in their day, but now almost forgotten.

A description of the Thames in 1893 says of this part of the river: 'At this point we begin to catch sight of the ubiquitous houseboats. They love the still lagoons and shady nooks that form a feature of the 'Royal river'. With their curiosities and vagaries of architecture in wood, their studies in colour, their pretty displays of plants, their dainty window curtains and the sounds and movements of their gay occupants, they delight the eye, and give a sense of comradeship to the solitary oarsman'.

Another solitary oarsman who rowed along here early one morning was that great nature writer Richard Jeffries, who lived for some time at Surbiton and was often on or along the river. Many of his writings contain records of his relationship with the area. In *The Open Air* (1885), he notes 'I paddled up the river; I paused by an osier-grown islet; it was the morning, and none of the uproarious as yet were about. Certainly it was very pleasant. The sunshine gleamed on the water, broad shadows of trees fell across; swans floated in the by-channels. A peacefulness which peculiarly belongs to water hovered about the river. A houseboat was moored near the willow-grown shore, and it was evidently inhabited, for there was a fire smouldering on the bank, and some linen that had been washed spread on the banks to bleach. All the windows of this gipsy-van of the river were wide open, and the air and light entered freely into every part of the dwelling-house under which flowed the stream. A lady was dressing herself before one of these open windows, twining up large braids of dark hair, her large arms bare to the shoulders, and somewhat farther. I immediately steered out into the channel to avoid intrusion; but I felt that she was regarding me with all a matron's contempt for an unknown man – a mere member of the opposite sex, not introduced, or of her 'set'.'

The owners of the last houseboats were given notice to quit from their moorings on Cigarette Island in October 1931. Within a few months nothing was left of these floating juggernauts to show their former glory.

In the latter part of Queen Victoria's reign and the spacious days before the Kaiser's War, the river functioned like a magnet to attract crowds of Londoners, who craved a respite from the dust and smells of the city streets and their ordinary humdrum workaday lives and escape for a while into the cleanness and tranquillity of semi-rural Thameside. Not all, of course, could afford the luxury of a plush houseboat or a suburban villa. Nevertheless, many decided that they were not to be left behind in the race for the river and fresh air. The fetish of the riverside week-end bungalow had started.

In a short time Cigarette Island and the adjacent meadows – the area once described by Pope as 'Those meads for ever crowned with flowers' – mushroomed with a bloom of motley home-made dwelling, a hotch-potch of caravans, crude bungalows and shanties, in an assortment of sizes, shapes, styles and colours. From wooden and corrugated iron shacks to travelling caravans, converted trams and buses, and even railway coaches, many had extraneous rooms added in piecemeal fashion, and from all kinds of building materials. An exemplification of vernacular architecture at its worst, the colony became known by locals as Venice on Thames.

These residences, graceless though they were, nevertheless had a link, so it was said, with Bluff King Hal, who once ruled the land in such stately splendour from the red brick pile immediately across the river. Legend has it that the court awoke one morning and found to its amazement that gipsies had arrived during the night and encamped on the meadows directly opposite the palace. Irate officials were just about to order them away, when Henry – obviously in one of his better moods – forbad them, saying that if the gipsies wanted to, they might stay as long as they wished, provided they did not make a permanent home there, and moved immediately they were asked to go. Apparently nobody ever asked them to vacate the land and, tradition says, they stayed. Certainly the original dwellings were all mounted on wheels. Although in later times they were sometimes fitted with electric power, piped water and even telephones, at least, theoretically, the stipulation that they hold themselves in readiness to remove at a moment's notice was strictly observed. All of which proves that pleasant legends may be told even of modern shanty towns and of sixteenth century absolute monarchs.

In the 1920s, when the possibility of controlling the environment through planning was beginning to be accepted, attempts were made to clear the colony and turn the land into an open space. In October 1926, the old East and West Molesey Urban District Council adopted a scheme to form all the land east of the railway, extending back to Summer Road and the boundary with Thames Ditton, into a public park, to curb the 'ever-increasing nuisance of caravan dwellers and occupiers of sheds'. The Council, however, could not at that time persuade either the County Council or any national body to assist in the purchase, and it was not until 1935 that Cigarette Island was finally thrown open to the public. The Office of Works, as it then was, decided to buy the land in order to preserve the view from, and of, the palace, and the freehold of the 'island' was transferred to the old Esher UDC.

From Cigarette Island one gets what is probably the finest view of that 'Structure of majestic frame, Which from the neighbouring Hampton takes its name'. See from this viewpoint the two distinctive styles of the palace – Wolsey's rich dark red brick, with its 'turrets and towers', and Wren's brighter red massive square block – are, as William Morris aptly put it, 'so blended together by the bright sun and beautiful surroundings, including the bright blue river which it looked down upon, that the beautiful building had a strange charm about it'.

Nathanial Hawthorn, that ubiquitous American, calls it 'a noble palace, nobly enriched ... it is impossible even for a Republican not to feel awe'.

OPPOSITE ABOVE: Cigarette Island in 1976, with Hampton Court Bridge in the right background; CENTRE: Hampton Court Palace from the Island, and BELOW: the Palace in 1911 – west entrance. ABOVE: Paddling was always a pleasure – for the young and for the young at heart. BELOW: On 20 April 1731, Sir James Thornhill created this 'View of Hampton Court Ferry from my lodgings' in pen and sepia wash – reproduced by courtesy of the Whitworth Art Gallery, the University of Manchester.

An Act for building a Bridge cross the River of
  Thames, from *Hampton Court* in the Coun-
  ty of *Middlesex*, to *East Moulsey* in the
  County of *Surry*.

## Cap. cxcvii.

An Act for making and maintaining Bridges over the River *Thames* at *Hampton* and *Shepperton*; and for other Purposes.   [21st *July* 1863.]

WHEREAS the making and maintaining of the following Bridges across the River *Thames*, with convenient Roads and Approaches thereto, would be of great public and local Advantage; (that is to say,)

First, a Bridge (herein-after called "*Hampton Bridge*") over the River *Thames* from *Hampton* in the County of *Middlesex* to the opposite Side of the River in the County of *Surrey*:

Second, a Bridge (herein-after called "*Shepperton Bridge*") over such River at *Shepperton* in the County of *Middlesex* to the opposite Side of the River in the County of *Surrey*:

And whereas the several Persons herein-after named, with others, are willing to make and maintain the said several Bridges, together with proper Roads and Approaches thereto, upon being incorporated into a Company for those Purposes: And whereas Plans and Sections showing the Lines and Levels of the said intended Bridges, and of the Roads and Approaches thereto, together with Books of Reference containing the Names of the Owners or reputed Owners, Lessees or reputed

[*Local.*]       33 N

LEFT: The Act of 21 July 1863 facilitated the erection and maintenance of bridges at Hampton and Shepperton, while RIGHT: that of 1750 authorised the first bridge at Hampton.

# HAMPTON COURT BRIDGE

From Cigarette Island there is a fine view of Hampton Court Bridge, surely one of the handsomest pieces of architecture on the Thames.

> But up the stream anent the village green,
> A bridge from Molesey Hurst the river spans,
> And pleasure boats of every size are seen,
> Where through the bridge, the breeze their tiny streamers fans'.
>
> John Stapleton (1878)

A ferry crossed this spot at least from Tudor times and probably much earlier. This, together with another running between West Molesey and Hampton, were appurtenances of the manor of Molesey Prior, and were acquired by the Crown with the manor in 1536. For some years after, the ferries were leased to various people independently of the manor. Thus in 1545 Hampton Court ferry was in the hands of Thomas Sheparde of Molesey.

By the middle of the eighteenth century this slow and cumbersome method of crossing the river had become so inconvenient and, at times of flood even dangerous, that Mr James Clarke, the lessee of the ferry, introduced a Bill into Parliament on 12 January 1750, to enable him to build a bridge across the river in its place. A petition in favour, signed by a number of influential gentlemen, was presented at the same time. The Bill passed both Houses and received Royal Assent on 15 April 1750. It enacted that 'it would be lawful for the said James Clarke to build a bridge' and to make and erect such highways and bridges leading to the same as may be considered necessary'. The bridge, designed and built by Samuel Stevens and Benjamin Ludgator, was opened for traffic on 13 December 1753. It was a peculiar, crazy affair of frail construction, with seven steep wooden arches. Not unpicturesque, it was reminiscent of the Chinoiserie of the Willow Pattern.

Of light construction, it soon fell into decay and, after only twenty-five years, was demolished to make way for a more substantial structure. The second bridge, on the same site, was also built of wood. Designed and constructed by a Mr White of Weybridge, it was opened in 1778. It was three hundred and fifty feet long and eighteen feet wide, with ten arches raised on piles and surmounted by a low parapet. It cost £7,000. A toll-house stood on the Middlesex bank, and on the middle of the downstream side was a stairway leading to a landing stage. This bridge was much more massively built than its predecessor and performed public service for close on a hundred years. However, for a number of years before it was finally demolished, complaints were voiced against it. One writer described it as 'ugly and hogbacked in appearance, it is neither safe or convenient for the traffic either above or below'. Several public meetings were held in East Molesey to press for a better bridge.

In 1863 the owner was forced to offer a new one by threats of Parliamentary action, and by May 1864 work had started. As it was being built on the same site, the old bridge had first to be demolished and, for a time, traffic had again to be ferried across the river. The bridge was completed and opened on 10 April 1865. It was constructed of wrought-iron lattice girders in five spans, resting on four pairs of octagonal cast iron columns sunk sixteen feet into the river bed, and on brick abutments. The roadway was twenty feet wide with a five feet wide pavement on the upstream side. The approach was between battlemented brick walls, one of which still stands on the Molesey side. A toll-house similarly built on the Middlesex bank is now part of the Mitre Hotel. The bridge was designed by Mr E.T. Murray, and cost £11,176.

With the continued rise in the volume of traffic that bridge too became inadequate. Especially on bank holidays and race-days at Hurst Park, and on the one occasion in each year – Whit Monday – when both these functions fell on the same day, the scene on the narrow bridge and approach roads was absolutely amazing. In 1905 it was reported 'towards mid-day visitors came in their thousands. The electric cars at times were well loaded. Thirty-eight special trains came down and over 40 were required for the return journey. Indeed at one period of the evening it is estimated that there was a crowd of fully 5,000 persons in the station yard awaiting their turn to pass on to the platforms. There were many thousands at Hurst Park, and though the attendance was not a record one, the general impression was the number of vehicles was larger than at any previous meeting. The police had a most difficult task in controlling the traffic, more especially at Tagg's corner and over the bridge, but thanks to good tact and temper all got safely through, and although there were many close shaves no serious accident resulted'. And this was on a day which started with rain.

In 1928 the Middlesex and Surrey County Councils obtained an Act of Parliament authorising them to construct a new bridge with the necessary linking roads and so demolish the old one. Work began in September 1930 on the building of the fourth and present bridge which included the demolition of the old Castle Hotel, the diverting of the river Mole into the Ember, and the filling in of the old Creek. A new road, connecting the bridge with the Portsmouth Road and the Kingston-by-pass, was constructed by the Surrey County Council. This is the road now known as Hampton Court Way.

The bridge is a handsome structure of ferro-concrete, the first Thames bridge so built, faced with hand-made red bricks and Portland stone, in the style of the 'Wren' portions of Hampton Court Palace. It was designed by Mr W.P. Robinson, county engineer for Surrey, with the collaboration of Sir Edwin Lutyens RA. It has three arches, the outers being 90 feet across, and the inner 105. The carriageway is 40 feet wide and the footpaths each 15. So each footpath is almost as wide as the complete width of the second bridge. The bridge was informally opened to traffic on Sunday 9 April 1933, when a procession of local people with torchlights and decorated vehicles passed over. The formal opening ceremony was performed by the then Prince of Wales (later Duke of Windsor) on Monday 3 July 1933. The original design provided for four kiosks or pavilions, two at each end of the bridge, which would have cost a further £8,000. These, after much controversy, were abandoned.

In 1938 Sir Edwin Lutyens flew over the bridge and wrote in his diary: 'my bridge from the air looks so much better than any others – why? I know but I shan't write it'. Which is rather a pity, because it would have been nice to have had the opinion of such an eminent architect, especially after he had whetted one's appetite so.

The Act enabling James Clarke to build the original bridge laid down that it should be built at his own cost, and permitted him to levy tolls on all users, from a half-penny for pedestrians to two shillings and sixpence for a coach drawn by six horses. These tolls were exacted, much to the chagrin of local inhabitants, until 8 July 1876, when they were extinguished by the Metropolitan Board of Works who bought the bridge for £48,000, part of the revenue received from the Coal and Wine Tax.

From the crown of the bridge a perfect vista is unfolded of the path our ramble up the river will follow. The eye swings round, from the wistaria-clad Mitre Hotel – looking very much the same as it has done for over three hundred years – past the trees on the left bank, and usually a row of motor boats moored at the Thames Motor Cruising Club, the weir and lock, with the tower of Hampton Church peeping over the trees, to the row of villas on River Bank. Standing here, one can sense what was in the mind of James Thorne when he stood on the same spot in 1849 and wrote: 'Looking up the river, you have a luxuriant prospect of the valley of The Thames, upon whose placid surface rest a number of well cultivated islets; and through the foliage so abundantly spread around peers out many a lowly and more than one lordly roof, and from many a chimney curls up the light smoke, gracefully contrasting with the dark hue and heavy forms of the trees, till it loses itself against the hazy sky; while in front Moulsey lock and weir, with the wide sheet of water rushing over it, impart strength and motion and a picture-like completeness to the view.'

The first Hampton Court Bridge, drawn by A. Heckel, and engraved by C. Grignion, was opened on 13 December 1753.

# Hampton Court Bridge.

## NOTICE.

# A PUBLIC MEETING

WILL BE HELD AT THE

## PRINCE OF WALES INN,

# EAST MOULSEY,

On SATURDAY, the 8th inst.,

AT 4 o'CLOCK IN THE AFTERNOON,

With a view to promote an application to Parliament for powers to provide better BRIDGE COMMUNICATION between the Parishes of HAMPTON AND MOULSEY.

**PUNCTUAL ATTENDANCE IS REQUESTED.**

Nov. 1st, 1862.

On 8 November 1863, the first steps were taken towards the better bridge that Parliament approved a year later.

ABOVE: In 1800 Thomas Rowlandson painted this watercolour of the second Bridge, with his customary dig at Society. BELOW: Fifty years later, another artist sketched this view from the Middlesex bank, clearly showing tollgate and house.

HAMPTON COURT BRIDGE.

OPPOSITE ABOVE: Tombleson published J. How's engraving in 1845 of the second Bridge, looking towards the Castle Hotel and East Molesey Mill. BELOW: By 1866 the third Bridge was a fit subject for yet another artistic endeavour. ABOVE: The third Bridge provides the backdrop to busy river commerce, a Thames barge in the foreground. BELOW: The Bridge is better viewed in this 1920s vista from the Surrey side.

ABOVE: 'Famous Thames Inns' of 1908 included this sunset study of the Castle Hotel, Mitre and third Bridge. BELOW: The riverbank at East Molesey boasted these battlemented walls on the approach to the Bridge, outside the Thames Hotel 'Luncheon, Dining and Tea Saloon'.

ABOVE: In 1908 Castle, Mitre and Thames Hotels shared the available custom, and then BELOW: the fourth Bridge came under construction.

ABOVE: The Prince of Wales opened the fourth Bridge on 3 July 1933.
BELOW: Earlier that year, the two bridges looked like this.

ABOVE: The fourth Bridge in 1952. CENTRE: Lutyens' original design included four pavilions, one at each corner.

BELOW: A dramatic shot of the final structure.

ABOVE: The embankment detail has changed on the East Molesey side as the Thames Hotel, now a Whitbread house, varies its message to 'Luncheons, Teas and Dinners'. CENTRE: The arms of Thomas Newland Allen were originally mounted on the third Bridge; they are now on the wall south of the present one. BELOW: Harry Tagg advertised 'Boats & Steam Launches For Hire' in 1904.

# T*HAMES* T*AVERNS*

As we come down from the bridge on the Surrey side, in front stands a restaurant and apartments on the site of the Joshua Tree, once Tony Roma's restaurant and bar, previously the Ferryboat Inn, and prior to 1969, the old Carnarvon Castle Hotel, c1860. Between Tony Roma's and the river, where now cars drive around the roundabout, at one time stood the Castle Inn, an ancient hostelry with a history going back to the early part of the seventeenth century. It was one of the most famous inns on the river, with a frontage right on the water's edge, and a landing stage so that boating parties could moor right by its front door. It was part of the Manor of Molesey Prior, which from the time of Henry was owned by the Crown, and was sold in 1816 under a special Act of Parliament to raise capital to buy Claremont as a residence for Princess Charlotte, daughter of the Prince Regent. In 1888 it was enlarged by the addition of an annex, to which the main building was connected by an ornamental covered bridge built over the road, and for which the owners paid a wayleave of one shilling per annum to the Molesey Council.

At the turn of the century its facilities were praised: 'Princes and their suites stay here, the famous cuisine and wines doubtless proving a great attraction. It is a prime favourite with the honourable and ancient fraternity of anglers. Racing men, who know a good thing when they see it, make the hotel a resting place, it being furthermore close to Hurst Park, Kempton, and Sandown'. The host, Mr Mayo, it says 'is known from John O'Groats to the Lands End'.

Unfortunately the Castle was in the way of the present bridge. The last thirsty customer was served on 15 March 1930, and the demolisher's pickaxe started its devastating work almost immediately after.

Fixed on the river wall on the site of the Castle we can now see a cast-iron plaque. This tablet, together with three other identical ones, was originally fitted in the spandrels of the third bridge – the iron one. It is embellished with the coat of arms of Thomas Newland Allen, the owner when the bridge was built.

The footpath here is terminated by a castellated brick wall with stone cappings, one of the original approaches built in 1865, and preserved as a listed ancient monument. Alas, however, that such conservation forces pedestrians to have to step out and walk upon a dangerous road. It is safest, therefore, to retrace our steps and walk down the stairs by the side of the bridge to the landing stage and along the water's edge. Immediately in front, at the foot of the first flight of steps, can be seen a heavy wooden door, which leads into chambers within the bridge itself. These form the basement for one of the pavilions which Lutyen's design intended for each corner of the bridge, the upper parts of which were deleted at the insistence of the Surrey County Council.

During Hitler's War this basement was used as a guard room by a piquet of Home Guards, whose duty it was to defend the bridge against all comers. How often the writer has stood outside this door at dead of night, complete with tin helmet, fixed bayonet, webbing pouches, and all the accoutrements of 'Dad's Army', doing his allotted two-hour stint, with only the insistent drone of the water rushing over the weir for company. But Oh! what a wonderful time for contemplation:

> 'From the twilight to the dawning,
> From the dusk to dewy morning,
> Flow dark river, weirdly gliding,
> Silent shadowy lands dividing'.
>
> *Delightful Thames,* Eliza F. Manning (1886)

And how pleasant to watch the sun slowly rising in the stillness of the morning. One felt, as surely Wordsworth must have felt, standing on yet another bridge over this self-same river:

> 'Ne'er saw I, ne'er felt a calm so deep!
> The river glideth at his own sweet will:
> Dear God! the very houses seem asleep;
> And all that mighty heart is lying still'.

The landscape between the bridge and Molesey Lock was considerably altered in the 1880s, firstly by the building of the Feltham Avenue, secondly by the construction of the Thames Hotel (later called The New Streets of London), and thirdly by the layout of the promenade. Feltham Avenue was so called from James Feltham, the former owner of the land, who was at one time the rentier of the tolls of the bridge. In 1835 Feltham complained to the Corporation of London because the lock-keeper was supplementing his income by keeping goats, and the animals were getting out and eating the hedges and plants on his land. 'I have no wish to deprive him of any pleasure (or profit if any) he may have in seeing these animals around him', he wrote, but still he hoped the Corporation would use its influence to prevent him from so doing. In 1889 the estate was called a 'row of genteel residences'.

The Thames Hotel was the brainchild of Mr Harry Tagg, member of a well-known waterside family, whose business acumen lifted them up from being the sons of a local waterman to the wealthy top rank of Thames entrepreneurs – helped, of course, by the circumstances of the day, by being in the right place at the right time, just when the exploitation of the river for pleasure was moving towards its zenith.

Mr Tagg had previously constructed a boat building works – the structure which stands between the hotel site and Feltham Avenue. He branched out from hiring small boats, to building boats, to hiring steam launches and culminating, in order to cater for all the needs of his patrons, in the refreshment business.

When the electric tramway came, bringing cheap travel to the metropolitan masses, and Hampton Court within a half-day's excursion, Tagg seized the opportunity to turn the upper part of the boathouse into a restaurant capable of seating three hundred people. 'The approach', it was described, 'is by a wide staircase from the road onto a balcony, and so into the room, the interior of which is painted white and beautifully adorned with flowers, palms, etc, and the view across the river is most pleasant. Mr. Tagg is nothing if not original, and in furnishing the place he has been fortunate in securing some of the handsome fittings from the Royal Aquarium and from 'Simpsons'. On the spacious balcony, teas can be supplied in the open air if required in full view of the river'.

One Thames guide says of the enterprise: 'It was a happy idea of his to have the whole place built for the express purpose of meeting the ever increasing needs of the boating public, who can thus have their aquatic and physical requirements catered for practically under one roof. For here we have an excellent hotel and restaurant, with commodious and adequate boat houses and premises adjoining and communicating – the whole built from the design of an eminent architect, aided by the practical knowledge of the essentials, the outcome of Mr. Harry Tagg himself. No expense or trouble has been spared to make the place comfortable and convenient to a high degree'.

The whole facade of hotel, boathouse and restaurant was covered by dozens of hanging baskets with flowers of every variety, a truly colourful sight. Even the land on the river side of the road down to the water's edge was laid out as a garden. The *Surrey Comet* of 2 May 1891 carried the announcement that: 'Mr. Harry Tagg of the Thames Hotel and boat building works, has made arrangements with the Molesey Band' (Yes! Molesey had its own band in those days) 'to play a selection of music this Saturday afternoon from 5 to 6.30 on the lawn of the hotel'. How pleasant it must have been then to have the musicians playing by the river without their melody being drowned by the eternal roar of motorised traffic.

Surely it was not for nothing that Mr Charles Dickens, the son of the novelist, wrote that Molesey 'is chiefly interesting to excursionists from the point of view of refreshments'.

The Thames Hotel was always known as 'Taggs Thames Hotel'; in fact, signs to this effect were displayed on the front, and today, although Mr Tagg has been dead for almost half a century, one may even yet hear it referred to by a local as 'Tagg's Hotel'.

At one time, when the river was considerably more used than it is today, it was almost impossible to walk along the slope down to the water in front of the boathouse, for row boats, skiffs, punts, and dinghies, all brightly varnished, padded with velvet cushions, and ready to be slipped straight into the water as soon as a customer appeared on the scene – usually a swain in flannels and straw boater, trying to impress his girl friend by his boating prowess.

The river has not always been as wide here as now. There was previously, close to the Middlesex bank, a tree-covered islet known as Wren's Island (not from the little bird, but because the famous architect lived in a house whose garden backed on to it). Between this island and the mainland was a narrow channel, described by Martin Cobbett, awakening from his sleep in the adjacent Mitre Hotel: 'First of all you become aware of a paddling, scuttering sort of noise – ducks busy in the shallow waters of a little creeklet under Hampton Court Bridge and then a good deal of quacking and wing flapping. You don't need to get out of bed to see what is going on amongst this industrious family party'.

Wren's Island was dredged away in 1931. Unfortunately this meant the felling of a row of lofty trees – whose beauty was commented on as early as 1794 and which were described just before they were uprooted as 'as fine a growth of timber as is to be found anywhere on the river'.

The promenade between the bridge and the lock was constructed by the Thames Conservancy in 1887, after reaching an agreement with the old East Molesey Local Board, and the freeholders of the Feltham estate. This laid down that the Conservancy would build a road forty feet wide and edge the slope with stone. The Local Board would lay down a footpath eight feet wide and plant an avenue of trees, consisting alternately of planes and limes. Unfortunately these trees have now all disappeared.

Along the promenade in the summer time there is often a number of craft tied up – motor cruisers, steamers, or barges, although fewer barges and more motor boats than there used to be. Lovers of T.S. Eliot will remember that it was whilst his barge was moored here, when 'The tender moon was shining bright', that Growltiger, the Bravo Cat, the Terror of the Thames, made his famous last stand when the barge was surrounded by his desperate enemies the Siamese, in their sampans and junks – as excitingly narrated in *Old Possum's Book of Practical Cats*.

ABOVE: Col Hodgson reviews the Surrey Bn Home Guard at Griggs Hill Green on 7 June 1942 – the author is second from the right. CENTRE: London United Electric Tramway no 296 at Hampton Court Bridge. BELOW: Somebody's parked his tricycle outside as he pops into Tagg's Thames Hotel and Restaurant.

# LOCK AND WEIR

In 1891 Joseph and Elizabeth Pennell made a literary tour of the Thames. They saw the river at the zenith of its popularity, and portrayed the scene in a work called *The Stream of Pleasure*.

Their description of the prospect at Molesey Lock is well worth recalling. 'At Moulsey Lock on Saturday afternoon and on Sunday you find everything that goes to make a regatta but the races. It is the headquarters of that carnival on the river which begins with June, is at its height in midsummer, and ends only with October. Not even in the July fetes on the Grand Canal in Venice is there livelier movement, more graceful grouping, or brighter colour. There may be gayer voices and louder laughter, for the English take their pleasure quietly. But I do not believe that men in their every-day amusements can show a more beautiful pageant anywhere. In the lock the water never rose nor fell without carrying with it as many boats as could find a place upon its surface. At the slide, where there are two rollers for the boats going up and two for those going down, there was always parties embarking and disembarking, men in flannels pulling and pushing canoes and skiffs. Far along the long cut, boats were always waiting for the lock gates to open. And on the gates, and on both banks, and above the slide, sat rows of lookers-on, as if at a play; and the beautiful rich green of the trees, the white and coloured dresses, the really pretty women and the strong athletic men, casting gay reflections in the water, made a picture ever to be remembered. However far we went, when we came back to the lock, it was only to find the same crowd, to hear the same endless grating of boats over the rollers, the same slow paddling out through the gates, the same fall of the water over the weir, and above all the other sounds, the monotonous cries of 'Tow you up to Sunbury, Shepperton, Weybridge, Windsor'. All the long Sunday afternoon the numbers of boats and people never lessened, though the scene was ever varying. And when the sun sank below Moulsey Hurst there was still the same crowd in the lock, there were still the rows of figures sitting on the banks; the men and horses on the road, the stray cycler riding towards Thames Ditton – and now, however, but so many silhouettes cut out against the strong light'.

It will be remembered that in *Three Men in a Boat* it was whilst passing through Molesey Lock that Harris recounted his harrowing experience in Hampton Court maze. Jerome K. Jerome's little frolic was first published in 1889. 'It is', he records, 'Boulter's not even excepted, the busiest lock on the river. I have stood and watched it sometimes, when you could not see any water at all, but only a brilliant tangle of bright blazers, and gay caps, and saucy hats, and many-coloured parasols, and silken rugs, and cloaks, and streaming ribbons, and dainty whites; when looking down into the lock from the quay, you might fancy it was a huge box into which flowers of every hue and shade had been thrown pell-mell, and lay piled up in a rainbow heap, that covered every corner'.

Even that sober and erudite historian of Hampton Court, Ernest Law, who wrote a three-volumed history of the Palace, was moved to write romantically of Molesey Lock: 'All day long on a Sunday, through Molesey Lock, just above the bridge, ceaseless streams, literally of hundreds of pleasure boats, each with their merry part of holiday makers, pass; while upon the banks, stroll throngs of young people, not perked out in "Sunday-go-to-meeting best", but men rationally dressed in easy shooting suits of flannels, and girls in neat and pretty lawn tennis or boating costumes'.

Reduced to the language of cold statistics, we learn from the *Surrey Comet* that, on the day of Molesey Regatta in 1895, no less than four thousand boats, one hundred and twelve launches, and eight barges passed through the lock, besides which, almost one thousand three hundred tickets were issued for boats proceeding over the rollers. What a day's work for the lock-keeper and his assistants.

It is doubtful if such spectacles will ever again return to the river; nevertheless, on a fine summer weekend, people still gather to lean on the rails, fascinated by the operation of the locks and sluices, and by the manoeuvres of the vessels as they enter and leave the basin. The scene, however, is very different from that observed by the Pennells. Muscular power has given pride of place to machinery. The operation of the lock is now controlled by electricity, and boats propelled by motors are far more in evidence, skiffs and dinghies almost non-existent. And alas, the gay summer frocks of the girls are now most likely to have given way to a pair of old jeans, and the bright blazers of the men to a tee shirt. Parasols and boaters have vanished, perhaps for ever.

Before the coming of railways the only economic method of conveying heavy goods was by water. Most of the country's commerce was therefore carried by sea or river, and later by canal. The Thames, quite naturally, was one of the chief highways for trade. A regular and extensive traffic of barges laden with goods such as coal, bricks, manufactured goods and the like, travelled up the river, towed by horses or gangs of men. They returned with timber, grain, vegetables and farm produce.

Barges might carry up to two hundred tons of merchandise per load and would require perhaps ten or twelve horses or upwards of fifty men to haul them upstream against the current. Many local men found work with the barges, both as boatmen and as manual haulers, or 'halers' a they were called. It was hard, exhausting labour and those employed were rough, tough men, who enjoyed a not too enviable reputation in the towns and villages along the river bank. In the early part of the seventeenth century Parliament passed several Acts in order to stop them from working on Sundays. An ordinance of 1641 enacted that 'noe person or persons shall use imploy or travell upon the Lords day with any Boate Wherry Lighter or Barge – upon paine that any person soe offending shall forfeit and lose the summe of five shillings for every such offence'. In 1662 a bargeman from East Molesey named William Bromfield was brought before the quarter sessions and charged that on 16 March, being Sunday, he did 'Sayle in his barge' from East Molesey to London, and did work, in evil example, against the statute, and against the peace.

The general expansion of national prosperity at the end of the eighteenth century gave considerable impetus to trade. In 1776 as much as 9,176 tons of goods reached Molesey from London. This was practically as much as that landed at Ditton, Walton and Sunbury put together (all at that time larger places than Molesey), so it would appear that these goods were not all destined for this locality, but probably off-shipped here for eventual onward transport to other places by road.

Although this method of conveyance was to modern eyes cumbersome, slow, costly, and at times dangerous, the alternative of land carriage, over the ill-made, ill-maintained, and ill-protected highways, with the attendant high risks and high insurance rates, was even more so.

Carriage by river, of course, was also beset by its own drawbacks – too little water at times, too much at others. With no weirs, there was virtually no control over the fickle flow at all. The river meandered at will. In some places it would crawl slowly over wide and shallow shoals; at others it would be narrow, deep and fast. At times of abundance the capricious water would overflow, cut a new channel and never return to its old bed at all. This in fact is how the aits, which form such a delightful feature of the river, came to be formed, and explains why parts of Surrey are to be found on the north bank and vice versa. For, although the river changed, the parish and county boundaries stayed in the centre of the old course. Under these adverse conditions river trade was a risky enterprise.

Zachary Allnut, the Secretary to the Thames Commissioners, in 1805, in a plea for something to be done to improve the state of the river asserted: 'the navigation upwards is attended at times with great difficulty, delay, expense, and danger'. The trouble seems mainly to have stemmed from the fact that after heavy rains, when there was an excessive downward flow, the barges being pulled upstream could not compete against the flood of water. Besides which, as Allnut further explains: 'The stream is so strong and violent; the fall or declivity of the water, removes the gravel at the bottom and sides of the river to partial places and creates shoals and obstructions to such an extent that in low water times, and in summer seasons, the navigation is for some months impassable for deep laden barges either upwards or downwards'.

It was these places, where the water was so shallow that barges sometimes had to wait for weeks at a time for enough depth in which to float, which were the main causes of complaint. With the expansion of river trade, and the extensive loss which the watermen sustained by this enforced inactivity, increasing pressure was brought to bear on the authorities for improvements to be made.

The Thames was one of the Royal rivers. From earliest known records the general jurisdiction over it, together with riparian profits, were a Crown prerogative. Richard I, to help restore the Royal coffers, depleted by his Middle Eastern adventures, vested the rights and revenues of the river in the City of London, in return for one thousand five hundred marks. This grant was confirmed by several later monarchs. The Lord Mayor and Corporation of London thereby held this responsibility with varying amounts of success and failure, until the Thames Conservancy was formed in 1857.

Some attempts to build weirs across the river, to hold back the stream and give sufficient depth of water, were made in certain bad places in the upper reaches. They were, however, mainly elementally wooden structures of stakes placed in the ground with planks laid across them to form a dam. Their weakness lay in the fact that they were only passable for vessels by removing some of the planks to form an aperture through which a flash of the pent-up water then flowed, on which a craft could ride fairly easily when going downstream, or with difficulty hauled upstream. This was known as a 'flash lock'. Obviously, the fall of these weirs and the depth of water which could be built up was limited. Negotiating them was an extremely hazardous operation. Each time it was done a large volume of water was lost. If too long a time was spent on the manoeuvre, so much water was let out that the level about was considerably reduced, and if it was done too often, the virtue of having a weir there at all was as good as nullified. Because of this, no weirs had been constructed below Staines, where the river was wider and the stream more violent.

The introduction of pound locks drastically altered the situation. The pound lock was simply a basin with gates at either end, into which vessels could be drawn and raised or lowered to the alternate level, easily, safely and with practically no waste of water. Weirs could now be made higher, giving greater depth of water above; the flow down the river could much more readily be controlled. Pound locks were said (like so many other things) to have been the invention of Leonardo da Vinci. In order to take full advantage of natural facilities they were usually placed between an existing island and the mainland.

In 1774 the Corportion of London obtained Parliamentary sanction to embark upon a series of improvements to the navigation, upon which they expended £10,000. In order to recoup this money and to bring in revenue for maintenance, a further Act was passed which permitted them to purchase the tolls which the various riparian owners throughout the river charged for allowing barges to be towed along the banks, and to commute them for one consolidated levy based on distance travelled and tonnage carried. Thus the rate from London was:

To Ditton, Hampton Court, Molesey and Hampton – 2d per ton; to Sunbury, Walton, Haliford, Shepperton and Weybridge – 3d per ton. In 1810 these rates were increased to 4d and 4½d respectively.

The opening years of the nineteenth century witnessed a flurry of activity. In September 1801 it was stated: 'that there is not sufficient water in the River to admit the Barges to pass in the lower part of the Navigation laden more than 3ft. in depth and that several Barges have lately been stopp'd in the Shallows about Laleham, Kingston, Hampton and Walton'. John Rennie, the celebrated engineer and designer of Old Walton Bridge, made a survey of the Thames and suggested certain improvements. He reported (amongst other things) that the river was particularly shallow by Platts Ait, which was borne out by another survey conducted by Zachary Allnut, which showed the depth there normally to be no more than 3ft 1in at the maximum. Rennie proposed that the passage on the Middlesex side of the island be stopped up by a weir and the Surrey channel dredged and a lock constructed. Apparently part of this suggestion was acted on, for in 1803, in an attempt to scour the main channel, it was reported that 'a weir in length 100 yards had been raised to divert part of the water of the back stream into the canal on the Surrey side.'

Alternatively Rennie suggested: 'In case it should be found, on an examination, that it would be easier and more certain to avoid this part of the river, a very favourable opportunity offers of making one or two side-cuts from above Sunbury Flats to near Hampton Court Bridge – A single cut, of somewhat less than three miles long, with a lock of six feet six, would completely avoid all this bad part of the navigation, and perhaps would cost less money than the other.' Apparently the latter scheme was the more favoured by the City Corporation, who became for a time canal-building enthusiasts. In 1807 they attempted to raise a Bill in Parliament to give them power to construct a certain number of waterways 'for the purpose of avoiding the places where the navigation of the said River is most obstructed.' At Molesey they proposed a cut starting by Platts Ait, bisecting the Hurst and running alongside Hurst Road, across Bridge Road and Cigarette Island, to rejoin the Thames again opposite Hampton Court Palace. For some reason, probably the opposition of the landlords, the Bill never materialised. Meanwhile the City seemed to have had a change of heart and to have come to the conclusion that they could never solve the problem without building weirs and pound locks.

In 1810 they introduced another Bill, which eventually passed into law and permitted them to build four locks – Chertsey, Shepperton, Sunbury and Teddington. The preamble recited that 'the navigation of the said River is still greatly obstructed and retarded, especially in dry seasons, by Shoals and Banks of Earth, Sand and Gravel, forming thereon, whereby a sufficient Depth of Water cannot be maintained', but went on that by the construction of these locks the 'Difficulties and Delays may be prevented.'

However, they soon realised that this scheme alone could not raise the water high enough above the shallows opposite Hampton Church and by Platts Ait. Therefore another Act was obtained to make, complete, and maintain another Pound Lock on the South West Side of the said River Thames, in the Parish of East Molesey, in the county of Surrey above the North West Side of Hampton Court Bridge, to be also navigable for Barges, Boats, and other Vessels, and which said lock shall be called Moulsey Lock – by which Means the Objects intended to be effected by the last recited Act will be further facilitated and more effectively promoted'.

Although Royal assent was given on 20 April 1812, construction work was not started for another two years, probably because the City was anxious for the four other locks authorised by the 1810 Act to be finished and fully commissioned before proceeding with Molesey. The lock was completed and traffic first allowed through on 9 August 1815.

It was one hundred and sixty-eight feet long and thirty feet wide, with a fall of six feet, and was constructed of wooden piles. A water-colour, now preserved in the British Library, shows the weir in 1827. It proves that it, too, was built of wood and by modern standards rather crude, having wooden panels with handles, rather like large paddles, which could be placed in position or removed at will to control the amount of water to flow downstream. At the same time a lockhouse was erected for the accommodation of the lock-keeper. The house is depicted in another water-colour in the same collection in the British Library, also dated 1827. It was Italianate in style, very similar in appearance to the one still in existence near Sunbury Lock. A plaque with the coat of arms of the City of London and the date 1815 was displayed at the apex of the forward gable. Down the centre of the front of the house was a panel on which was a table of the tolls chargeable on all classes of vessels using the lock, together with a list of navigation rules, and the words 'MOULSEY LOCK'. The present author can just remember (he was barely seven years old when this house was demolished) looking at these words and being extremely amused at what seemed to young eyes highly unorthodox spelling. On either side of the house was a wall with gates leading to the rear, where there were probably stables, for it must be remembered that barges were still horse-drawn when the lock was built, and most lock-keepers augmented their not too liberal stipend by using their premises as change-houses.

The first lock-keeper was a man named John Nash, formerly a butcher in the City of London. However, fate decreed that Nash was not to enjoy the situation for long. In June 1820 he took time off to watch the races on Molesey Hurst and, haplessly getting into the path of one of the racehorses, was run down and killed.

The keepers originally received a salary of thirty-two shillings a week, but through the years this was several times reduced until in 1854, owing, it was said, to the loss of trade due to the coming of the railways, the job was advertised at eighteen shillings. For that the keeper had to be available, or pay an assistant, to pass boats through the lock both day and night. Their lot, nevertheless, was not entirely a monotonous round of opening and shutting gates and raising and lowering water. The busy river traffic coming and going inevitably brought diversions, amusing and dramatic, lighthearted and tragic. A number of tales have found their way into official archives, where they may be found hidden among other more prosaic chronicles. The lock-keepers also found time to augment their earnings by other means, and not always in the most honest fashion. In 1829 the then keeper was discharged after casks of ale and cheeses mysteriously disappeared from barges as they passed their way through Molesey Lock.

As boating became more and more the pastime of ordinary people – people who had little or no experience of the river or of the hazards it held – so the number of accidents around the lock increased, bringing more trouble to the overburdened keepers especially from boaters venturing their craft too near to the ever-rushing, ever-sucking maelstrom of the weir stream. Almost every year during the hey-day of river life the local newspapers record at least one fatal occurrence at Molesey weir, and in 1877 it was announced that a man was to be stationed in a boat above the lock at busy times to warn oarsmen away. Mishaps still occurred.

Another misadventure occasioned by unskilled hands was caused by tying the boat up too tightly and forgetting to allow for the water's rise or fall. In the early days, as pleasure boats paid no toll, those in charge were expected to operate the lock themselves, not an easy task for those unused to it. One incident which happened in the 1830s illuminates the official attitude towards this kind of traffic.

Two childrens' maids and their charges, who were being taken on a trip by a man, were proceeding through the lock. The man closed the gates and was attending to the sluices but, as the water fell, the boat, which he had tied up without sufficient length of loose rope, upended. Only after a desperate struggle were the frantic nursemaids able to throw the children onto the bank and clamber ashore themselves. Although complaint was made to the City authorities that no assistance had been offered by the lock-keeper, the argument was made that the keeper was not responsible for working the lock for any vessel under three tons.

As the balance between commercial and non-commercial traffic shifted, due to changing methods of transport and the economic forces of the mid-nineteenth century, the attitude of the Corporation was forced to change with it. Barges became fewer as river trade gave way to the competition of the new-fangled iron railways and macadamised roads. Leisure time increased, first for the new middle classes and later for all, and the vogue of taking pleasure on the Thames became increasingly the fashion of the day. A select committee was appointed to report on the preservation of the river, which declared that 'the ancient employment of the Thames as the waterway of a considerable commerce has dwindled to an almost insignificant point, whilst the pleasure traffic on the river, in consequence of the conversion afforded by the railways, and of the ever-increasing tendency of the great population of the Metropolis to seek on the river exercise and recreation, has in the inverse ratio increased; and it has grown to such dimensions on holidays, and, indeed, throughout the summer months, as to render some legislation with a view to preserve the character of the river as a place of free but reasonable recreation and enjoyment'.

In view of the loss of tolls from the decline of the barges and to maintain the navigation, new sources of revenue were demanded. Therefore, in September 1866 the Thames Conservators, who had taken the river over from the City of London Corporation, extended tolls to include pleasure boats. Rates were fixed at boats with one pair of oars 6d, with two pairs of oars 1s, steamers 2s, and houseboats 2s 6d.

As the boats now paid duty, lock-keepers were obliged to assist in their passage through the lock, and were forbidden to accept gratuities for so doing, which they had been allowed if they helped when no toll was charged. In spite of this, in July 1869 David Phillips, the Molesey lock-keeper, was reprimanded by the Conservancy for asking for tips from the owners of pleasure craft.

In 1871, in order to reduce the multitude of rowing boats, punts, skiffs, and the like, which cluttered up the lock at busy times, roller slides were added above the main basin. This greatly facilitated the passage of little boats from one level of water to the other, and without the tedium of having to proceed through the lock itself, which was thereby left free for larger vessels, bringing about a considerable saving in time and patience for both types of craft.

Some of the people with small boats sought to escape paying the lock tolls, and save time as well, by lifting their craft out of the river, carrying it along the towing path, and depositing it back on the water on the other side. Some even went so far as to pull them over the weir – a perilous practice. In fact, as the law then stood, this was perfectly legal, as the Act only demanded a duty from those who actually passed through the lock. By the 1870s the Conservators were losing so much revenue by this stratagem that they had a special clause written into their Act of 1878, by which craft paid the toll 'for passing through, by, or over a lock.' Thereafter, this type of evasion seems to have been stopped.

Throughout its life the lock was continually improved, as engineering techniques themselves improved and better methods of construction were discovered. In the early 1850s, owing to the anticipated lowering of the water in the reach below the lock, due to the construction of the intakes of the waterworks at Long Ditton, it was considered advisable to dredge the river and lower the depth of the lock. These works were completed during 1853. The weir, which had fallen into a dilapidated condition, was rebuilt in 1859. During 1882 it was again rebuilt, as part of the remedial works necessitated by the great flood of 1877. This time two large portions of Ash Island were purchased and dredged away, the spoil being spread over the rest of the island to raise its level. The tail of the island was cut away to enable the weir to be lengthened, thereby facilitating an increase in the flow over it, and enabling the flood water to get away more quickly, at the same time lessening the danger to passing boats. Several fatal accidents had occurred due to the narrowness of the channel and the rapid stream, which drew small boats towards the weir.

On 2 June 1906 the lock was reopened, after a complete reconstruction lasting some nine months and costing £14,000. Its length had been increased to two hundred and sixty-eight feet, making it the largest on the Thames after Teddington.

During 1915, due to heavy rains, the water rose and fell several times in the Lower Thames Valley, causing considerable flooding. A large breach was formed in the lock island between the weir and the lock. Temporary protective measures were taken immediately, but the continuous high level of the water caused the damage to extend, with the result that a portion of the concrete retaining wall of the tumbling bay fell in. Before putting permanent repairs in hand, the Conservators mooted an interesting idea. They suggested constructing a small lock on the site of the breach, instead of filling it in, which would be used by single vessels, thereby reducing the delay caused by opening the big lock and also reducing the amount of water wasted in times of drought. They offered to undertake the work if the Metropolitan Water Board would contribute half the cost. To this the Board agreed, but the Local Government Board insisted that the work should be postponed until after the war. As, however, the repair of the damage required immediate attention, the proposal was abandoned, and steps taken to permanently fill in the breach.

Also during the First War, defects in the fabric of the lockhouse became apparent. In 1915 the Conservancy carried out some repair work, but it became obvious that major improvements would be necessary. Total collapse of the building was prevented by shoring up the sides with timber, but complete rebuilding was considered essential. As soon as practical after the War, a plot of land adjacent was obtained and the present house was built, and first occupied in 1926.

Like many other establishments, the lock underwent adaptations to survive the perils of the 1939-45 War. The Petroleum Board had set up an oil installation just above Sunbury Lock, to save incoming tankers the hazard of running the gauntlet of German guns along the French coast to the London Docks. They discharged their precious cargo at Avonmouth, whence a pipe-line was laid direct to the Thames, where the fuel was stored in subterranean tanks before being pumped into barges to be taken on to London. It is estimated that, during an average day, about fifty of these barges, fully loaded, passed through the lock on their way to the metropolis. Had one of them sprung a leak, or been attacked by enemy aircraft, a whole sheet of highly flammable liquid would have spread over the water and collected around the lock. As a precautionary measure, therefore, the vulnerable wooden gates were entirely sheeted over with thick steel plates, and special fire-fighting apparatus was housed nearby.

In 1959 the lock was completely restored and modernised, with electric controls for the gates. The passage of vessels was restricted to three days a week to facilitate this.

Before leaving the lock and continuing our ramble up the towpath, perhaps we can spare a moment to recall a few lines from a poem written by a lady named Eliza F. Manning, and published in 1886 in a volume called *Delightful Thames*. The poem, *A legend of Moulsey Lock*, is not particularly well-written, and its subject – the fickleness of the fair sex – is a trite theme; nevertheless it re-emphasises the part the river played in Victorian recreation:

> 'A Legend of Moulsey Lock
>
> Alone, a lady waits on the lawn,
> A lady blithe as the bright May morn
> 'Til a boat glides up to the daisied sward,
> With a find young fellow of course, on board
> Then down she trips to the bank and cries –
> "My dearest Charles, what a pleasant surprise!"
> And he answers, "Dora, my dearest dear,
> How exceedingly lucky to find you here".
> 'Tis a beautiful morning to be afloat,
> And he hands her tenderly into his boat.
> With her Japanese sunshade, her wraps, and her fan,
> An acceptable cargo for any young man
> To stow into his boat, and to carry away,
> And have all to himself for the best of the day.'

But alas! the fitfulness of passion – the path of young love never did run smooth. The 'best of the day' turns out to be very short indeed. The lovers quarrel, she espies another:

> 'That intolerable dandy, young captain Furneaux,
> By himself in a boat, that would nicely hold two.
> He's a sociable fellow, and keeps by their side,
> and he chats with the lady as onward they glide.
> 'Till they come to the lock, when he bids them adieu,
> As he's not out for long, and don't mean to go through.
> Then the lady said, "Charles, I prefer, if you please,
> To get out on the bank, and wait under the trees;
> I won't go through the lock as I usually do".
> But she don't look at him, but Captain Furneaux.
> "I'm so tired of sitting – you've no need to stare –
> You go through with the boat I can wait for you here".
> All humble obedience he hands her on shore,
> And whispers, "My Dora, forgive, I implore".
> Then he passed through the gates they are closed – it is done.
> "Now he's nicely shut in," laughed the lady, "What fun."
> And tripped down the bank, and Captain Furneaux,
> Said frankly, "I wish to return, and with you".
> High the Captain's moustaches and eyebrows are raised,
> As he whisks her away. They are off! What a shock
> It will be for poor Charles t'other side of the lock!"'

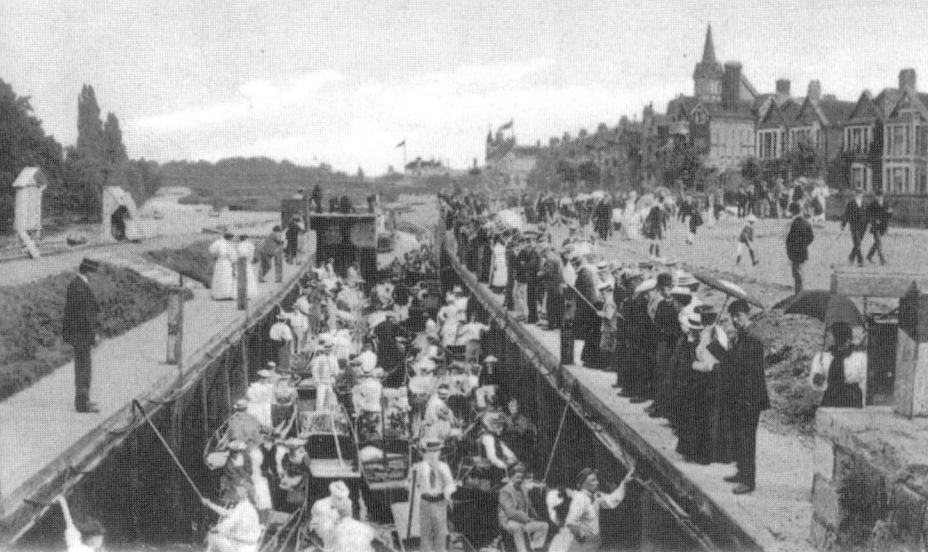

ABOVE: Molesey Lock, CENTRE: the 'Stream of pleasure', BELOW: from the Bridge.

45

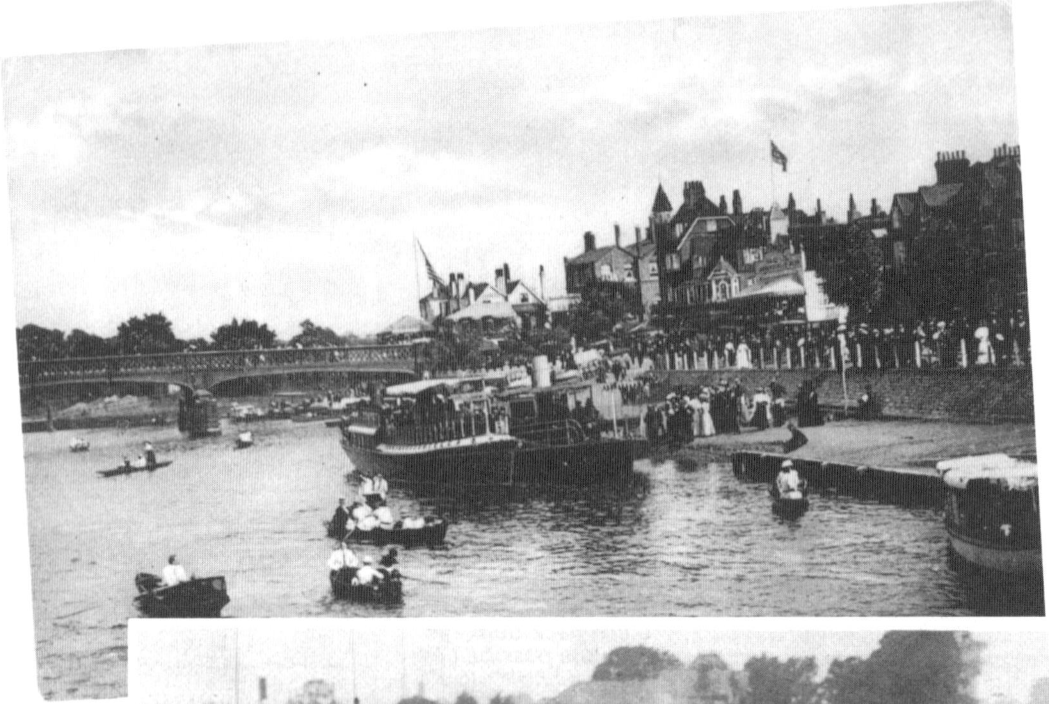

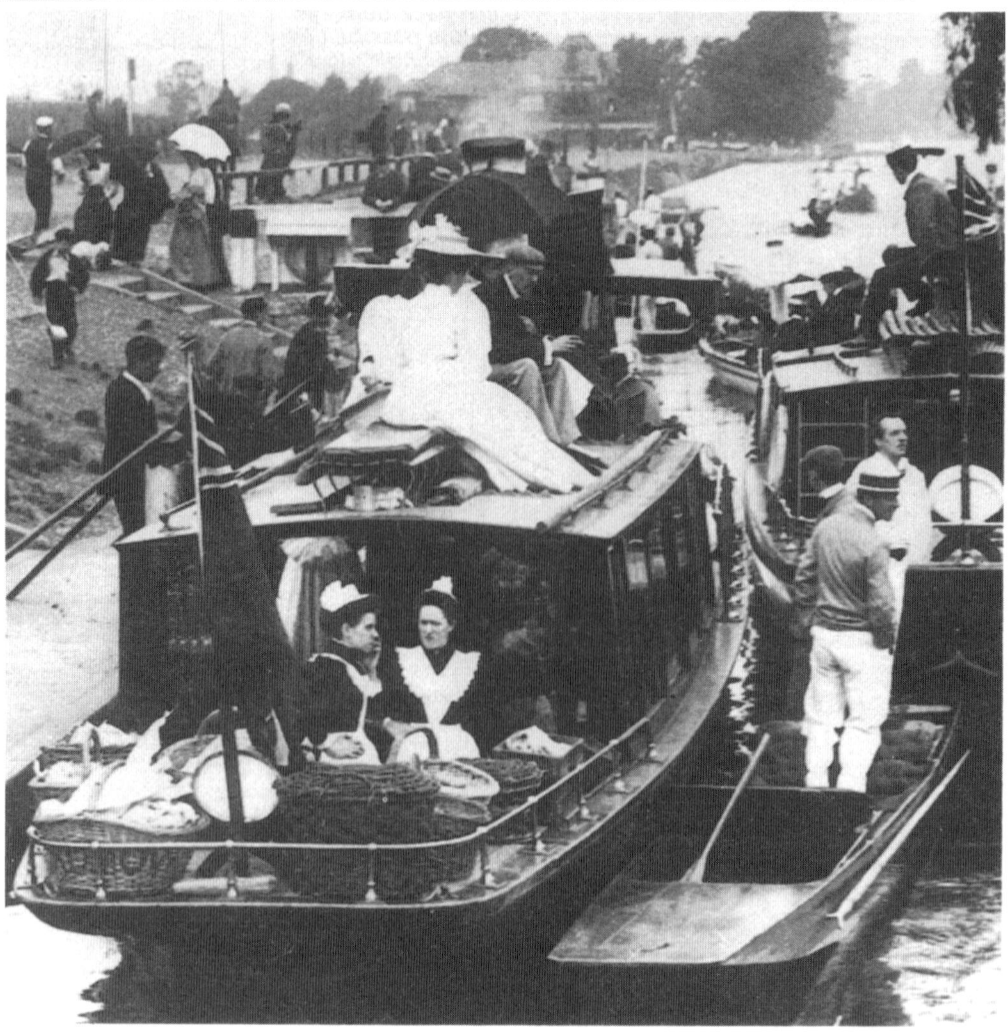

OPPOSITE ABOVE: A crowded riverscape, with pleasure steamers, bustles round the third iron Bridge. BELOW: This smart 1896 launch party have taken their maids aboard to serve their every whim – including their picnic repast.

Molesey Labour Party had no need of maids – they had one another for company in 1926, in substantial numbers.

Molesey Lock: the Rollers, in 1905.

ABOVE: The Lockhouse, East Molesey in 1827, by E. Hassell. BELOW: The same artist painted this watercolour of Molesey Weir that year.

ABOVE: The Weir in 1913, CENTRE: another view, and BELOW: flowers at the Lock in 1979.

# FLOODS, FIELDS AND FINES

As we pass away from the lock it is worth while just glancing at the wall on the Conservancy offices, where there are two cast-iron plaques, originally fixed on the side of the old lockhouse, showing the height to which the water rose during the floods of 1821 and 1894. On the wall beneath the lock-keeper's office is a similar one for March 1947. The overflowings of the river, the bane of their existence to Thames-side dwellers, are often commemorated in this way. Until a short time ago there was such a mark on the side of the Thames Hotel, the level of the great flood of November 1894. Yet another, on the old Ferry House which stood opposite the Hurst, likewise perpetuated the memory of 1774. These marks are a useful guide in determining the relative heights of various floods; thus the flood of 1821 was higher than that of 1894, but less than 1774's.

Molesey residents know only too well the calamity of an over-abundance of water. They wait with apprehension when snows suddenly melt on frost-hardened earth, or when the region is covered by prolonged static precipitation (to use the meteorologists' jargon). For they know full-well that all that liquid must inevitably run through their valley on its journey down to the mighty sea. Strangely enough, however, Molesey, or at least most of it, does not flood from the Thames. A perceptible ridge of high ground runs from Cherry Orchard to Palace Road, effectively protecting the village from the Thames. Molesey's big danger is, of course, the river Mole. Thus the 1947 flood, marked by the plaque on the lock, which caused great havoc in the Thames valley by the rapid thawing of deep snow in the upper reaches, was hardly seen in Molesey. Conversely, the heavy downpour in early September 1968, falling mainly on the Surrey Hills and carried away by the Mole and Wey, totally submerged most of Molesey, yet caused hardly a stir higher up the Thames.

We can picture in our mind the scene here during the last two decades of the nineteenth century. Victorians discovered the Thames and flocked to it in their thousands as never before. The author of *Three Men in a Boat* who often used to row between Richmond and Staines says 'At first we used to have the river almost to ourselves, but year by year it got more crowded.' He describes most vividly the scene around Molesey Lock: 'On a fine Sunday up the stream, and down the stream, lie waiting their turn, outside the gates, long lines of still more boats; and boats are drawing near and passing away, so that the sunny river from the Palace up to Hampton Church, is dotted and decked with yellow, and blue, and orange, and white, and red, and pink. All the inhabitants of Hampton and Molesey dress themselves up in boating costume, and come and mouch round the lock with their dogs, and flirt, and smoke, and watch the boats, and altogether, what with the caps and jackets of the men, the pretty coloured dresses of the women, the excited dogs, the moving boats, the white sails, the pleasant landscape, and the sparkling water, it is one of the gayest sights I know of near this dull old London Town.'

The holiday atmosphere along the towpath is recalled by Martin Cobbett, a one-time resident of Molesey and kinsman of the noted Rural Rider – William Cobbett. In his

*Wayfaring Notions* (1906), he writes: 'I can see Jerry Hawkes' (a champion light-weight boxer) 'up on the barge walk just above Molesey Lock, when we put him on to a try-your-weight machine pitched on the tow path. Jerry knocked the whole apparatus bang into the river.'

It would amaze, or perhaps amuse, today's young generation if, by the wave of a good fairy's wand, they could be transported some sixty or more years back to witness the animated scene on and along the Thames any sunny summer Sunday evening. Motoring was in its infancy and the riverside was the general escape from every-day cares. Almost the whole locality put on its Sunday best and went for a stroll along the towpath.

The author well remembers the ritual: we children in front, Father, an upright figure striding out with his walking stick, with Mother by his side, bringing up the rear, stopping every few yards to exchange comments and gossip on the weather, politics, sport, any and every subject one fancied, with whatever friends and acquaintances one met, or to watch the ceaseless flow of craft on the river, or listen to a merry party on a houseboat, launch, or steamer, singing and dancing to the latest popular tune emanating from the large brass horn of a gramophone. Sometimes, as a special treat, we would even take the steamer ourselves – sailing down to Kingston, and riding back on the tram, on steamers such as *Viscountess, Marchioness,* or *The King*.

That indefatigable chronicler of nature in all its facets, Richard Jeffries, loved this part of the river. 'Just above Molesey Lock', he writes, 'in the meadows beside the towing path, the blue geranium or crane's bill grows in large bunches among the mowing grass in summer. It is one of the most beautiful flowers of the field: after having lost sight of it for some years, to see it again at last seemed indeed to bring the old familiar country near London.'

Alas Jeffries' meadows no longer exist. At one time they had been 'Lot Mead', perpetuating the old manorial custom by which the tenants were apportioned their share of the meadow's crop by a process of drawing lots. Then they were occupied – behind a rather hideous fence – by the Upper Deck Swimming Pool. Opened in 1936 by a private company, the first pool in England to draw the water which filled it from the very ground on which it stood, it was then managed by Elmbridge Borough Council, who bought it in 1969 for £15,000, less than half what it originally cost to build, and spent another £36,000 modernising the changing rooms, showers and filtration plant. Right pleasant it was on a hot summer's day to see the pool full of happy chattering youth, surrounded by colourful spectators. It closed in the mid-1990s, to be replaced by a housing development.

During the appropriate months of the year along the bank of this reach, 'The patient angler takes his silent stand. The pliant rod now trembling in his hand.' At one time Molesey was the headquarters of the Thames Angling Preservation Society, and trout were captured here less than a century ago; in fact, it was the lowest part of the river usually accepted as suitable for this type of fishing. A fish ladder was added to the weir in 1864 to help the fish swim upstream. In those days a number of local people earned their living as professional watermen, fishing, hiring boats, and assisting amateur fishermen. Most of them lived in the cottages in Bridge and Creek Roads. The families of Milbourne, Davis, Watford, Martin and Tagg were well-known and respected along the Thames. Nowadays river fishing is entirely a recreation for amateurs, the fish taken, I am told, include barbel, jack, perch, roach, dace, pike and gudgeon, and in the tumbling bay, heavy tench may be caught.

Just before the First World War the Molesey Urban District Council, showing much more foresight than it usually displayed, drafted a forward-looking plan to create a public park alongside the Thames from the lock to Hurst Park. This was joyfully reported in *The Times* in August 1913: 'A scheme for increasing the amenities of the River Thames was brought before the urban district council of East and West Molesey at its meeting yesterday by the chairman Mr. J. Ray. The proposal involved the construction of a boulevard by the riverside, extending for a distance of about half a mile, from Molesey Lock, to the boundary of the district opposite Hampton. The undertaking is expected to add greatly to the attractions of the district. The present scheme is to acquire – voluntarily if possible, but if not by compulsory powers – a strip of land varying in width from 30ft. to 64ft. adjacent to the towing path and commanding a fine view of a picturesque stretch of the Thames, with Hampton church in the distance, and Garrick's Lawn and Temple and Tagg's Island and the "Karsino" in the foreground. The belt of trees standing on the land will not be disturbed and it is proposed that the boulevard shall be so laid out as to make it one of the most delightful spots on the banks of the river. The District Council very heartily approved the scheme, and instructed the clerk to take all the necessary steps to obtain powers for the acquisition of the land.'

The 'necessary steps' included the obtaining of an Order from the Local Government Board permitting the compulsory acquisition of the land, which was signed and sealed on 6 March 1914, and confirmed by special Act of Parliament in the same session, receiving Royal Assent on 8 July.

The plan was supported by the Thames Conservancy Board, and received approbation from Mr Tom Burns, the President of the Local Government Board. Unfortunately, and to their everlasting shame, it was not entertained with the same enthusiasm by certain people in Molesey. The scheme would have involved an addition of twopence (less than one new penny) to the rates – surely a small price to have paid for such a magnificent extension to the recreational amenity of the district. Even this insignificant amount was too much for a section of the electors. They formed a residents' association to fight the plan, stood some of their members for election to the Council and, after a bitterly fought contest, won. The Molesey Scheme was defeated and dropped. Oh! if only the electors had had the foresight of their Council, they would have invested their twopences in a worthwhile piece of property which would now be valued at several million pounds. A short while ago, less than two acres of this self-same land was offered to Elmbridge Borough Council for £340,000.

Opposite the old Upper Deck site, the Thames races over the weirs continuously, whipping the river in the tumbling bay below into a boiling, writhing mass of froth. The weirs connect an island, of some four acres in extent, which is called Ash Island, probably from the trees with which it is covered. It has known many names – Garrick's Lower Eyot (from the famous actor, whom we shall meet again later), Mr Clay's Ait, Anglers' Ait, Harvey's Ait, Ashen Ait, and (by far the most delightful this) Robinson Crusoe Island.

At one time the island was much lower than it is today, and was often overrun by floods. In 1844 it was reported as being 'washed away', and some years later the owner complained to the Thames Conservancy about the erosion. After the 1877 floods, parts were dredged away and spread over the rest of the island to raise its level, a process which was repeated during the navigation improvements which accompanied the erection of the new Hampton Court Bridge in the early 1930s.

About 1850 a man named Joseph Harvey, who was then the tenant, attempted to open up the island as a refreshment centre, catering for boating and fishing folk. A wooden beerhouse was built, adjoining which were a skittle-alley and tea gardens. The whole went under the grand title of 'The Anglers' Retreat.' Although the premises were somewhat tumbledown, it was said of it some years later it 'provided good dinners and other accommodation at prices which at Thames-side hotels are now things of the past.'

Harvey, however, seems to have fallen foul of the local constabulary for consistently selling beer on a Sunday during morning service, which was against the law. The inspector at Hampton police station tried several times to catch him but, as he complained, 'he himself had been over to the island, but being so tall he was easily observed.' Therefore, he had to employ a subterfuge and, dressing up two of his men in disguise, sent them over to the island; the hapless host was caught red-handed and hauled before the magistrates. Harvey pleaded guilty, and said he was a poor man, and the people came to the island and imposed on him, and if they fined him he did not know what he would do. Nevertheless the beaks fined him £5 with 8s 6d costs. The next Sunday the inspector sent another two constables, again suitably attired, and again he was caught selling beer out of hours; again he pleaded guilty, again he said 'he was a poor man and if they fined him he did not know what he should do', but again they fined him £5 with 8s 6d costs. Yet again on the following Sunday two policemen arrived on the island, dressed as gardeners, and for the third time Harvey found himself in front of the justices, but this time he pleaded not guilty and brought witnesses to prove his case; notwithstanding he was still found guilty but, as apparently they were not too sure, this time they only fined him 50s with 16s costs. Whether this tipped the scales and frightened him off or whether he set up an improved early warning system and was never caught, or even whether the inspector thought him so incorrigible he gave up trying to stop him, is not clear, but he never seems to have graced the dock again.

During the great freeze-up of February 1855, when the river was frozen solid, the following advertisement was posted:-

'Glorious News!
A sheep to be roasted on the Thames, near the Angler's
Retreat, between Hampton and Hampton Court, on Friday
afternoon, February 23rd, 1855, between two and three
o'clock, and the public are invited to partake of the same.
Two barrels of superior ale will be supplied at the same time.'

The day of the sheep roasting started off apparently with the frost as intense as ever but, by the time midday arrived, a swift thaw had set in, and the unfortunate caterer had scant time in which to sell his roast mutton and 'superior ale' before the whole ice melted away.

For a number of years the enterprise seems to have paid off, but after some bad experiences of flooding the proprietor deemed it expedient to transfer the complete undertaking upstream to the higher and drier land of what is now called Tagg's Island. He obtained a lease, and there constructed premises built of brick.

In 1866 Molesey Boat Club was formed and Ash Island became its headquarters.

OPPOSITE: Upper Deck swimming pool in 1971. ABOVE: In 1894 the Thames flooded the Feltham Estate and Lockhouse. CENTRE: Plaques on the Conservancy Office wall mark the flood levels of 1821 and of 1894. BELOW: Boating at the Upper Deck was fun for children (including the author's).

ABOVE: Tom Milbourn's café and fishing tackle shop advertised in 1900 and BELOW: looked sadder in 1974 – it has since been renovated.

# *M*OLESEY *B*OAT *C*LUB

The story of the founding of the Boat Club is said to be that a number of young men of Molesey formed a crew which they called 'The Argonauts', and tried to join up with the Kingston Rowing Club, but the latter refused them membership, whereupon they called a public meeting at the Prince of Wales Hotel, which agreed to subscribe towards the establishment of a local club. Very soon a constitution was adopted and officers elected. Within two months it was reported 'The new boat house being built on Mr Clay's ait just above the lock is fast progressing towards completion, and when it is finished the club will be well provided with the necessary requirements in that respect. The number of members is on the increase'.

The budding club quickly secured a reputation along the river. By 1874 they were competing at Henley, and in the following year reached the final of the Grand Challenge. The zenith of their success appears in the early 1890s. In 1890 they reached the finals of both the Thames and the Wyfold. They won the Thames in 1891 and the Wyfold in both the two following years.

By the end of the century the clubhouse on Ash Island became too cramped and inaccessible. The club, therefore, resolved to abandon its insular home and build grander and more commodious premises on the mainland. In 1899 a piece of land by the towpath was leased from Mr Kent.

In the same year Mr James Abram Milner, who had been born and lived all his life in Palace Road and was honorary secretary to the regatta for over ten years, died, and it was resolved that the new boathouse should be erected as a monument to his memory. The *Surrey Comet* of 26 June 1901 records that 'The new boathouse which has been erected on the Surrey shore, adjoining Tagg's boathouse, to the memory of that thorough sportsman, J.A. Milner, was formally opened on Saturday. The building is a thoroughly substantial structure, measuring outside 70ft. by 26ft., and there is ample room for the housing of a large collection of racing craft. On the upper floor there is a handsome dining or club room opening out on to a deep balcony along the whole front of the building. Behind the club room there is a commodious dressing room, fitted with every convenience, with lockers, shower bath etc. From the front a capital view up and down the river can be obtained, while the western side overlooks the Molesey C.C. ground and Hurst Park race course. The club can now boast of having one of the largest and most convenient headquarters on the river'.

This building is still the headquarters of the club. Every weekend on the river bank young rowers can be seen carrying eights from the boathouse down to the water. Along the river lithesome backs sway and stretch to orders barked through a megaphone by coaches cycling correspondingly along the towpath.

The scene was described much more lyrically by Richard Jeffries: 'The oars are dipped farther back, and as the blade feels the water holding it in the hollow, the lissom wood bends to its work. Before the cut water a wave rises, and repulsed, rushes outwards. At each stroke, as the weight swings towards the prow, there is just the least feint depression at its stern as the boat travels. Whirlpool after whirlpool glides from the oars, revolving to the rear with a threefold motion, round and round, backwards and outwards. The crew impart their own life to the boats; the animate and inanimate become as one, the boat is no longer wooden but alive'.

In 1867 the club, though yet only just over one year old, ventured to run its first regatta. Supporters rallied round to subscribe prizes, and the *Surrey Comet* proudly announced: 'Thursday next will see the first regatta held under the management of Molesey Boat Club. The committee are working hard to do all they can to bring it off with success: should they fail it will not be from any want of zeal and energy on their part'. Alas! zeal and energy and a hard-working committee were apparently insufficient, for the enterprise was not repeated the following year. Nor in fact was an open regatta arranged by the club itself again.

After a lapse of a few years an association was formed, quite separate and distinct from the boat club, but naturally having strong affinities with it, for the specific purpose of organising an annual amateur regatta at Molesey. The first meeting under the auspices of this body was held in July 1873 and, save for three seasons in the late 1870s and the dark years of the two world wars, has been conducted ever since. The actual course over which the races have been rowed and the place of the finishing enclosure have changed positions several times over the years.

The holding of regattas by amateur rowing clubs really evolved out of the contests of skill organised between the various professional watermen who plied their craft on the river. Molesey was noted far and wide for the proficiency of its boatmen – men who made their living from the river – and a Watermen's and Fishermen's Regatta had been held here for many years prior to the amateur regatta. In 1861, for instance, the *Surrey Comet* reported the event: 'The annual regatta came off with great success on Thursday last, when the fineness of the weather and the attraction of the day induced one of the largest assemblages that have ever congregated on a similar occasion. The only drawback to the amusement of the day arose from a melancholy accident occurring from the wadding of a small gun exploding, whereby Richard Tappling, 78 years of age, had his left arm broken, and a lad named Cowdy was severely bruised above his right elbow. The sports concluded by the renowned Pig Hunt which was conducted by A. Kilfoyle and Thomas Tagg, and was gallantly won by T. Whatford, whose brother Charles, the celebrated amateur Blondin, walked for the fourth time across the river on a rope 1¾ inches in circumference at an altitude of 40 feet, in a most successful and courageous manner'. In 1885 Molesey Watermen's Regatta was described as 'rough enjoyable fun, tempered with good-humour and gaiety of spirits all round'.

In later years, at the peak of the river's popularity, at least two other regattas were held annually in Molesey: a Boat Club Regatta, restricted to members of the boat club and an Invitation Regatta, which was really a water frolic with novelty races, canoes, gondolas, and coracles.

The reputation of Molesey Amateur Regatta grew until its stature on the Thames ranked second only to that of Royal Henley. It was the event of the season, not only for the competitors, but for the entire district. By the middle of the afternoon, except for a space left in the centre of the river for the rowing course, boats of every description – skiffs, dinghies, punts, launches – were packed gunwale to gunwale as tight as it was possible to be.

In the period following 1888, after the racing had concluded, and darkness had begun to fall, a remarkable spectacle took place. Spontaneously, the owners of the launches, which were already dressed overall with flags and bunting, lit them up with brilliant illuminations, and all the small boats were imaginatively covered with ornamental decorations, or made up to represent swans, paddle streamers, fantastic animals or anything else that could be conceived, with their occupants in suitable fancy dress. Then all the craft would parade up and down the river like so many fireflies, in a sort of water carnival procession, for the benefit of the crowds on the towpath and the parties on the houseboats.

The houseboats, too, were all cheerfully illuminated with countless Chinese lanterns, fairy lights, and chandeliers, their rays flooding and gaily hung flower baskets with a glitter of vari-coloured lustre. As far as the eye could see was a fairyland of twinkling animated light, a glorious festival which was known as the Venetian Fête.

The pageant in 1895 made such a vivid impression on one newspaper reporter that he almost ran out of superlatives: 'The Venetian Fete. Following the regatta and later in the evening one of the most successful river fetes ever held in Molesey was carried out under the most favourable conditions. The illuminations on the river and along the banks from Hampton Court to Hampton were a grand spectacle, and the sight presented to the vast crowd was a splendid one and almost beyond description. The concourse of people who assembled to witness the pageant was very large. People seemed to come in shoals along the banks of the river, and long before the twilight deepened the thoroughfares were thronged with eager and anxious sightseers, who when they were able to witness the magnificent sight that was soon placed before them were unanimous in their applause and praise. Looking upstream from the lock the spectacle was charming. The river was thronged with all kinds of boats. In some instances the occupants of craft had taken a great deal of trouble to contribute their share to the festivities of the evening. All along the Barge-walk were fanciful strings of Chinese lanterns making the bank stand out very prominently in the darkness. Thomas Tagg and Son at their boathouse on the Surrey shore always have a large display. They were very successful in their efforts on the present occasion. The whole building seemed radiant with coloured lights. The front was covered with Vauxhall lamps. Near the boathouse special reserved enclosures were to be found in one of which the Molesey Band played some excellent selections of music. The old quarters of the Molesey Boat Club were effectively treated while several of the houseboats were one mass of illumination, notably Mr H.H. O'Hagan's "Grantully Castle", moored at the head of the tumbling bay; "The Shop Girl" stationed off St. Albans; Mr H. Hewitt's magnificent houseboat "Satsuma", at the foot of Platt's Ait, and Mr Wrestler's neighbouring houseboat "Siesta". The river gardens of South-view, Hampton, had received effective treatment, while the premises of the Thames Valley Sailing Club, Hampton, and the lovely river lawn of St. Albans house was one of the spectacles of the evening, arranged as it was in many coloured tints and hues. As usual a bridge of lights was suspended from Taggs Island to the Barge-walk, and a similar string was also festooned from the club-house to the end of the lock. On the Barge-walk Mr W.H. Smith of Hurstside had very prettily arranged fairy lights and flowers on a very effective background of cork. "River-view" was tastefully decorated with Japanese lanterns. The Castle Hotel was finely treated, balconies, gables, windows, archways, etc, sending forth scintillating lights. The Carnavon Castle, with its new buffet, presented a very effective appearance, small lights and flowers being used as decoration. In fact everybody seemed to have the one thought, and that was to make the fete a grand success'.

Out of the Venetian Fête developed the custom, which continued up to the start of the Second World War, of holding an evening firework display. The fireworks - rockets, Catherine wheels, coloured lights, set pieces, the lot - were lit at the head of Ash Island, just opposite the Boat Club headquarters.

We as small children lined the river bank, arriving soon after tea in order to procure a place in the forefront with a good view of the island. There we whiled away the time watching the sprightly scene. As the daylight gradually faded (not quickly enough for us of course) the crowd got thicker and thicker and noisier and noisier. From the lock to the cricket club the towpath became a seething mass of good-humoured humanity. The river too was jammed so tightly with boats of every variety that very little of the water could be seen, and it would have been easy to walk right across from the shore to the island without wetting one's feet at all.

Eventually the time arrived for the pyrotechnics to begin, the first firework was lit, and, as if by magic, a hush descended upon the assembly, a hush which was only punctuated during the whole performance when a rocket which had been shot into the air perforated into a myriad buds of falling light, or a series of coloured fires was lit among the trees, giving the island the aspect of a fairy glen – then the entire throng broke into one concerted impulsive lingering sigh of 'ahhh!'. At other times all was silent until the last set piece heralded the conclusion of the performance, and the crowd broke into the singing of the national anthem. Then the dense multitude gradually melted as the people shuffled slowly away, the boats queued once again to pass back through the lock, leaving the celebrations still going on in the clubhouse, the parties on the houseboats, and the blaring of the roundabout organs at the fair on the cricket ground.

The official programme of the Molesey Amateur Regatta in 1898 and 1901 was authenticated by the secretary's signature.

**1867 - 1967**

**MOLESEY**
**CENTENARY**
**REGATTA**
UNDER A.R.A. RULES

Saturday, July 15
1967

SOUVENIR PROGRAMME
PRICE 2/-

**Gentlemen, as Sportsmen, are earnestly requested by the Committee to do their utmost in helping to keep the Course clear.**

LEFT: The centenary Regatta programme in 1967 has acquired a nostalgic air after 21 years. RIGHT: Molesey Boat Club at Barge Walk with ABOVE: a request from the 19th century Regatta promoters. BELOW: Fishing was fun at the Weir in 1907.

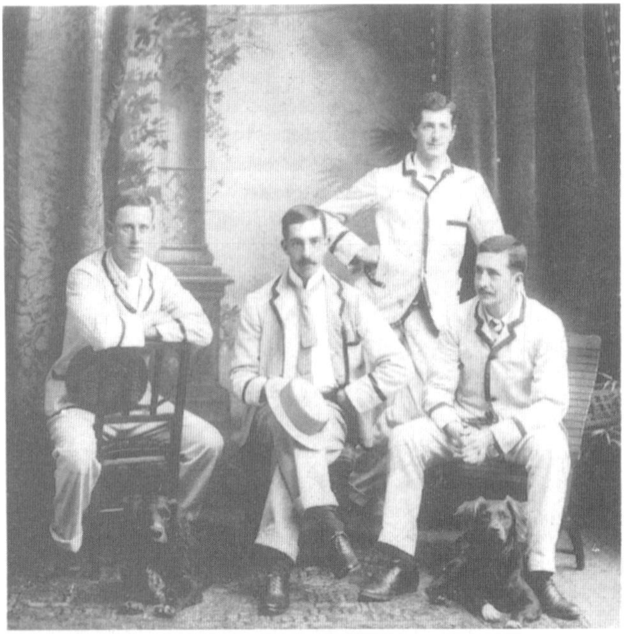

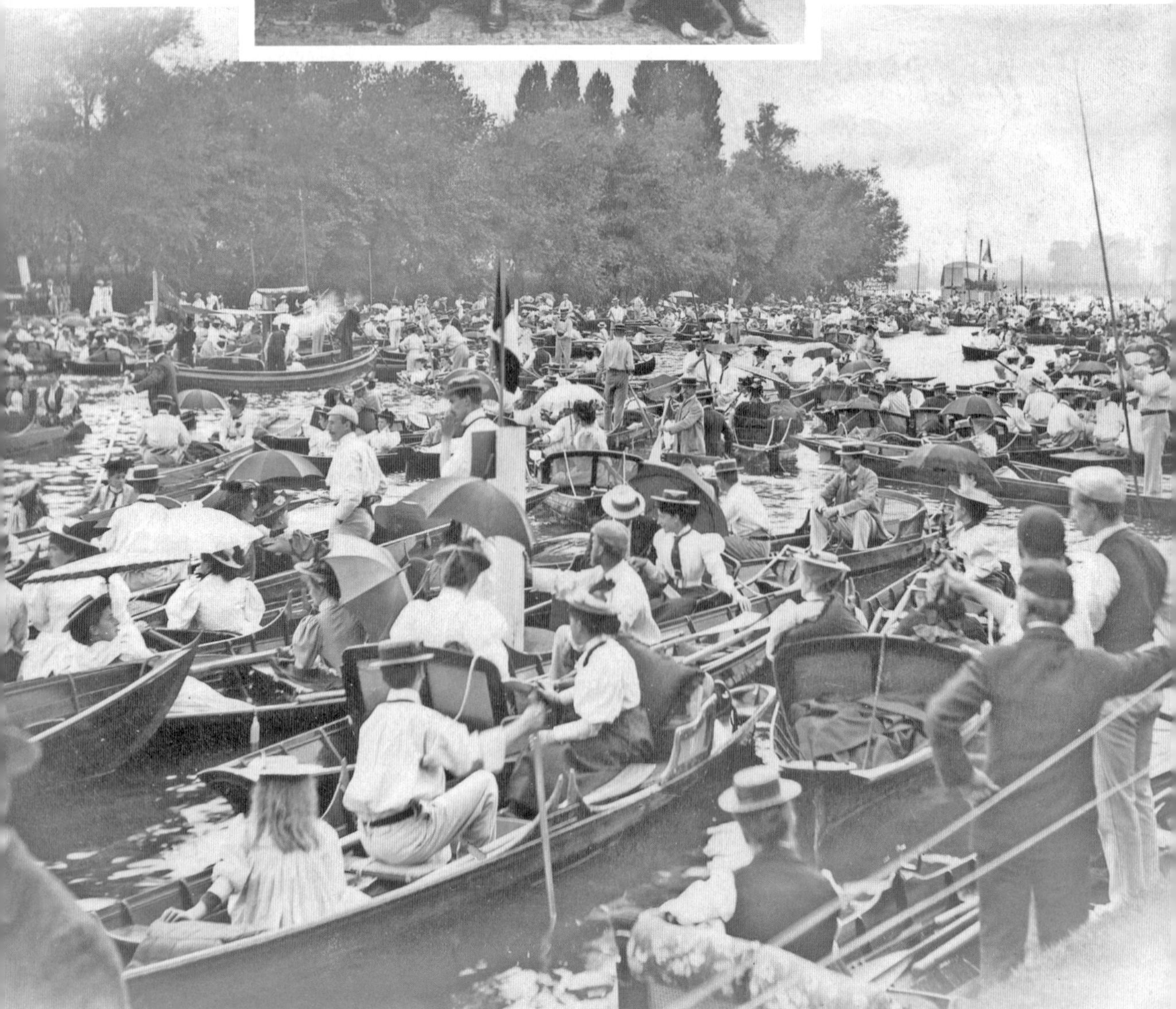

OPPOSITE ABOVE: Molesey Boat Club Senior Fours in 1891: left to right – A. Piper (3), C. W. Kent (stroke), N. Block (Bow) and H. A. Block (2). BELOW: Molesey Regatta, 1894 – water, water everywhere and not a drop to spare.

In 1894 the Regatta crowd seethed in front of Garrick's Villa and Temple – and in 1956 C. W. Kent recognised himself in the foreground of this picture.

ABOVE: In 1913 the Regatta had thinned out a little – or perhaps it was simply better organised. BELOW: In 1904 it was certainly more crowded by Garrick's House.

# TAGG'S ISLAND

The piece of water separating Ash Island from Tagg's used to be called the Hog Hole. This name is often used on the Thames for a deep channel between two islands, although no reason is given. Probably, however, it is derived from a now obsolete word *'How'*, meaning a concave hollow. Wright's *English Dialect Dictionary* gives 'How-hole – a hollow, a depression'. As this was also sometimes spelled *'Houghle'*, a further progression to 'Hog-hole' would be an easy step.

As we stand here on the towpath and look across the river between the two islands, we can see on the Middlesex bank what appears to be a Swiss chalet. This is, in fact, an authentic fragment of Switzerland. Dismantled from its native soil in the latter part of the last century, it was brought over to be erected on this site in what was then the grounds of a large house called 'Riverholme', which stood, until a few years ago, a little way downstream.

A genuine piece of Swiss architecture might be considered incongruous on the shores of an English river, but such is the variety of the Thames scenery that even this characteristically continental structure dissolves harmoniously into the prospect. Unfortunately its status has gradually diminished since it was first raised here. From a summer house in a private garden it became a restaurant, and is now incorporated into a boat-building yard.

Tagg's Island was once Crown land, part of the manor and honour of Hampton Court. It has had several names during its history. In the early eighteen hundreds it was called Walnut Tree Island, and this is the name under which it usually went until it was acquired, about 1850, by Francis Jackson Kent, a Hampton lawyer and property speculator, who bought and developed much of the land of East Molesey in the middle of the century. After this it was often called 'Kent's Ait'.

When Kent purchased the island it was populated by a number of squatter families, who made a precarious living by cutting the osiers, or willow rods, which once grew in abundance and which they peeled, bleached in the sun, and made into baskets. These were not the sort of people Kent wanted on his island. He had bought it as an investment. It had to earn him money. The squatters paid no rent. Off the island they would have to go, and Kent evicted them lock, stock and barrel.

One of the people who was born and lived on the islands was a Mrs Hester Lock, who died in West Molesey in 1932 at the age of 102. She then had over 50 descendants still living, and the profusion of this family name in Molesey is undoubtedly due to her.

Legend has it that some of the people expelled were gipsies, who left their insular homes reluctantly, cursing Kent roundly, and saying that nobody connected with the island would ever prosper. Unquestionably no enterprise which has been ventured on the island has flourished for very long, although, as far as Kent himself was concerned, the malediction seems to have been so much water off a duck's back. He certainly prospered, and died worth a considerable fortune.

Soon after Kent acquired the island he appears to have rented a part to Joseph Harvey who started and ran the 'Angler's Retreat' on Ash Island. He now moved this entirely to the larger island. Kent also leased a piece to a boat-builder called Thomas George Tagg, thus formally introducing the island to the name which has stuck to it ever since.

The Tagg family was renowned along the riverside for its prowess on the water. They seemed to have immigrated to East Molesey from Thames Ditton in the early part of the last century. In 1841 two branches of the family occupied cottages in Bridge Road close to the Albion Inn. By 1906 a description of Surrey could mention Molesey as 'a noted port of pleasure boats, and the name Tagg, that has taken such banyan - like root here'.

The family was so well-known on the river that one was posed the question 'Why is the Thames like a shoe lace?' The reply to that was 'Because it has a Tagg [tag] at each end'.

Edward Jesse, the well-known naturalist and author, one of the founders of the Thames Angling Preservation Society, who lived at one time in the house which is now West Molesey Vicarage, wrote in a book called *Anglers' Rambles* in 1836: 'John Tagg, the worthy fisherman lets out boats and punts at Hampton Court, provides rods, lines and baits, and waits upon those anglers who employ him, with equal civility and attention. He is moreover one of the King's watermen, and manages a punt better than most men on the river. He is a great favourite in the neighbourhood'. This John Tagg is said to have a handsome fishing rod which had a brass plate on which was engraved: "Admittedly the chief among fishermen and propellers of punts, knowing full well the deepest waters of the Thames and its locks, especially acquainted with the springs of Diana and the streams that water the paradise of Bushey. A man known throughout the regions of the earth! A man, with scarcely his equal among mortals! An incomparable man! To him now, Brinsley and Frank Sheridan, the exponents of his praises, have endeavoured to offer this token of their admiration. Presented to John Tagg, for his many virtues and transcendant talents in Fishing, By Sheridans, Brinsley and Frank'.

Another author who mentions him was the sporting writer Martin Cobbett, who described him as 'one of the finest, handsomest men I ever saw. Jack the ever free and frolicsome, who once whitewashed a donkey on the fifth of November, bundled the creature into a barber's shop and wanted him shaved, saying that he was already lathered'.

Thomas George Tagg was known as Tom Tagg junior, to differentiate from his father, Tom Tagg senior, who was also, naturally, a waterman, and was brother to Harry who founded Tagg's Thames Hotel by Hampton Court bridge. Whilst Harry and another brother, Sam, took over their father's business, Tom junior branched out on his own. He was appointed a Queen's waterman at the age of 21, and started building boats on the island. He had sufficiently succeeded by 1868 to reconstruct the boathouse, with larger space for boat-building and storage, and with residential accommodation above, into which he moved with his wife and six-year-old son, George, from their cottage near his father's in Bridge Road.

His energy was boundless, his initiative and business acumen considerable. He pioneered new methods of boat construction and boat letting. Cobbett says he 'was an inborn genius in devising craft, from a skiff to a steam launch. He was an honoured member of the Institute of Naval Engineers'. He also characterised him as 'One of the best friends I ever had. A rare good sort, a fine sportsman who could walk, run, and fight when fighting meant P.R. business, and would take on anyone who upset him, weight of no consequence'. (P.R. = prize ring).

His industry got larger and larger - and so did the size of the boats he created. By 1869 he was already constructing launches, a line from which he probably gained most repute. During six years in the 1880s he was awarded twelve gold medals when his launches were shown at exhibitions in both Britain and France. The list of customers and patrons looked like several pages from Debrett. For some reason he always christened his most prized launches *Princess Beatrice*. The first of these caused a sensation at Henley in 1887 when it appeared carrying the Prince of Wales and other British and foreign Royals. It eventually went to the Baltic for the use of the Russian Czar's family. The third, built in 1897, was at the time considered the handsomest launch on the Thames. Catering for up to 150 people it was described as 'luxuriously furnished and fitted. It has a spacious Promenade Deck, and contains Ladies Saloon, large Dining Saloon, Lavatories and Piano. Specially suitable for first class parties, and patronised by members of the Royal Family'.

Soon after his first arrival Tagg obtained a lease of the whole island, including the cultivation of the osier beds, and kept pigs, poultry, and cows as well – a veritable little farm. His enterprise knew no bounds and each undertaking seemed to flourish. In September 1872 he took over the licence of the Angler's Retreat, and entered into his new role of mine host with willing enthusiasm. Soon he was discussing with Kent, his landlord, the provision of a larger and more imposing hotel, to cater for the increased numbers of people using the river.

Within a year the new hotel was built. It was a much larger and more elegant structure than the old Angler's Retreat, with an entrance hall, bars, coffee room, smoking room, and bedrooms for guests, each with a verandah with views out over the river. The old beer licence was transferred, and shortly after, a full wine and spirit licence was granted.

Ripley's *History of Hampton* mentions that 'in excavating the foundations, which went seventeen feet through uninterrupted loam soil, the workmen came upon several interesting zoological remains, among others what were pronounced (by Professor Owen) to be the skull of an extinct species of goat, and the jawbone of a large boar's head, relics which mutely but eloquently explain the history of the island'.

Before long Tagg had transformed the island from a back-water beer house into a popular pleasure resort. It become a Mecca for society; Royalty, nobility, and millionaires rubbed shoulders with theatrical, artistic, and literary folk, swells, squanderers, and shadowy gents of all kinds. 'During the season', it was said, 'its well-kept lawn, dotted with chairs and tables, presents a very gay scene, thronged with well-known people, members of the theatrical and musical profession predominating. Especially is this the case at week-ends, when celebrities are to be seen in great numbers'. The Duke and Duchess of Fife, Sarah Bernhardt, and some others of whom mention will be made later, were particularly fond of the island. In 1885 it was described as 'truly a lovely and interesting place'.

Tagg's Island, too, was yet another convenient anchorage for the ubiquitous houseboat. From the 1880s the perimeter of the island was fringed with ranks of these exuberant floating juggernauts. A long line of vessels, their verandahs were bedecked overall with gaily striped and tasselled awnings, their railings, balustrades, and ornate carvings, freshly painted each season in rich and striking colours. Viewed from the towpath it was indeed a glittering sight. Perhaps the most dazzling of all was Mr John Bradford's *Gipsy*. A large houseboat, near the centre of the line as seen from the Molesey bank, it was covered all over with brilliant tiers of hanging baskets and tubs filled with vivid vermilion geraniums and other flowers of every hue.

On a balmy Sunday evening, as darkness was spreading, the brightly coloured lanterns were lit, sending shafts of rainbow light streaming and reflecting across the shadowy water. The melodious tones of an old-fashioned brass-horned gramophone came from the upper deck. The very vessel itself seemed to burst into life. All around, on the Molesey towpath and in countless punts, people stopped and listened. It was surely such a scene which inspired Thomas Love Peacock, who lived at Shepperton, to write:

'While melting music steals upon the sky,
And softened sounds along the waters die,
Smooth flow the waters, the zephyrs gently play,
Belinda smiled, and all the world was gay'.

These free concerts continued for a number of summers and were much appreciated by the people, who used to make a special journey each Sunday down to the river to listen and to look. Unfortunately the owner of the island considered that it drew customers away from the hotel, and told Mr Bradford that he must stop giving the concerts or he would have to remove his houseboat from the island. This order almost broke the kindly owner's heart, he so enjoyed the pleasure his music gave to people. He could not bear to stop on the houseboat without playing the gramophone so he decided to sell the *Gipsy* and get right away from the place where he was much admired and had for many years done so much to brighten up the scene.

There are still floating homes to be seen moored around the island, but now they are mostly converted motor boats or barges. Yet one or two old houseboats linger. They are, however, mere shadows of their former selves. Stripped of their grandeur, like dowdy dowagers they squat majestically on the water, dreaming of the expansive glories of their youth.

In the earlier days, when the water was not contaminated with petrol waste nor the air polluted with jet-engine drone, the riverside was sweet and serene. Among those who could afford it, the fashion was to have a Thames houseboat, in which to relax in pleasant surroundings, to give gay parties, and to taste awhile the blithe Bohemian life. Molesey was a magnet which drew the great and the not so great, the famous, those who hoped for fame, and those to whom fame could come one day.

In the latter category two in particular stand out. The first was a young Scottish journalist, writing under the name of Gavin Ogilvy, who was just beginning to make a name for himself, and who hoped to make an even greater one. He did. Under his real name – J.M. Barrie – he became world-known as the creator of the eternally youthful Peter Pan. The second was a music hall actor called Fred Westcott.

James Matthew Barrie arrived in London in the mid-1880s after having served some time on a Nottingham newspaper, and his articles start appearing soon after in metropolitan magazines. With a kindred spirit and fellow Scot – J.L. Gilmour – he hired the houseboat *Arcadia,* and in July 1887 we find him extolling the virtue of houseboat life in an article in the *British Weekly,* a periodical which was usually of a much more sedate nature, as its subtitle, *A Journal of Social and Christian Progress,* implies. Barrie livened it up. In his writings of houseboats he says:

'A more delightful holiday for a family, I cannot easily conceive; and for a man who has to run up and down between his summer quarters and London, there is nothing to approach it. They are of all sizes. Mine was for a party of half-a-dozen persons. It was sixty-five feet long by about thirteen feet broad, and in appearance was simply a wooden house built on a barge. It consisted of five rooms – a saloon, three bedrooms and a kitchen. The saloon was much the largest room, some seventeen feet long. It was the full breadth of the boat, and a passage ran from it to the other end, off which doors opened into the bedrooms and kitchen. The ceilings were as high as in an ordinary house, and the deck was seated to hold fifty people. But one of the charms of a houseboat is that it makes a backwoodsman of you for the time. It is an utterly new life, because you leave conventionality behind you, and it has an educating influence in showing you how little man really needs here below'.

'All houseboats should be as pretty as swans on the water, and most of them are, for no one would care for houseboat-life who is not romantic in the sun, and if you are romantic you love the beautiful, and so you cannot help making your home on the river picturesque. It is easily done, for flower-pots make a garden of the deck, and what is prettier on a summer's day than a hammock swung beneath a Chinese umbrella? The river is so willing to meet you half-way in your desire to make it pretty in the moonlight that it takes the lighting of a fairy-lamp as the signal to unroll its panorama. A boy struts up the towpath with a penny whistle, or drifts down on his back in a dinghy, and the place and the hour make a musician of him. Skiffs flash by in a blaze of coloured lights. Listen to the water whispering among the reeds. Who said Nature slept in the night?'.

'All communication with the land is by small boat. You have a punt or dinghy for this purpose. The houseboat is anchored between trees near the bank of the river which is private ground, the public thoroughfare, or towpath, running along the opposite bank. For obvious reasons it is well to lie within easy distance of a village. Telegrams are brought to you (or rather to the opposite side of the river, where you must cross in your dinghy for them), and the shopkeepers, being largely dependent on houseboats also send purchases up the towpath. Letters must be called for at the post-office, unless a special arrangement is made'.

'The life is quiet but not monotonous, for no day is quite like another. Hundreds of boats pass by every hour, from shrieking steam-launches to Canadian canoes, and on Sundays there is a wonderful procession to church that blocks the landing stage and brings craft together that were built on many waters. Saturday is set aside for visitors who are going back by the last train but stay till Monday, and there are dells and clumps of trees all the way up the river, and all the way down it, where ladies love to pic-nic. I don't know what a houseboat would be like in winter. No one does. I think of trying it'.

In the quiet of these idyllic surroundings Barrie's pen worked with demoniac fury. He had thoughts of producing a novel, and wrote in another magazine - *The St. James's Gazette* - 'I see that I laid my plans with care when I moored this houseboat against the island at Moulsey. My purpose is to get on with my novel, doing the writing in the saloon and the thinking on the island; the western half of which is a straggling stretch of green hooped around with houseboats. Here and there is a tree to knock your hat off as you go round thinking. A more perfect place for planning a romance could not be imagined'.

Barrie's training as a journalist had impressed upon him the importance of maintaining the highest degree of authenticity and attention to detail in his writings, and in his early works the themes are inevitably based on the scenes and characters which surrounded him, which he knew well and which he could portray precisely. In his heroes we can easily recognise Barrie himself, a quiet ambitious young man, but not yet quite sure of himself, especially with the opposite sex. Tagg's Island and the houseboat *Arcadia,* as well as featuring in numerous magazine articles, became the setting for two chapters of his first full-length novel - *When a Man's Single* and the whole scenario for his first successful play - *Walker London.* Later, in a eulogy on the pleasure of tobacco smoking entitled *My Lady Nicotine,* the *Arcadia* was remembered yet again, and his favourite brand was given the name Arcadian Mixture.

In *When a Man's Single* Barrie also entitles one of the inns The Angler's Retreat. Obviously the name of the island's first hostelry was still remembered around the place.

Even Tagg's little farmyard, which had then dwindled to the presence of a solitary cow, was brought in to enliven the proceedings. He explains in a little piece called 'Round the Island', the style of which is somewhat reminiscent of another Thames writer - Jerome K. Jerome, 'Near this point lies a houseboat in blue and yellow, called the Victory; and in the

Victory our pretty girl lives. I say our pretty girl because we all belong, more or less, to the island; also because she really is a pretty girl. Gilmour thinks so too; though this is hardly worth mentioning, as his opinion on such a matter is of small value. Once we saw the pretty girl looking in our direction; and Gilmour who is the last man in the world to interest a woman, thought that she was looking at him. This amused me a good deal at the time; for I have a strong sense of the ridiculous and now I never see that houseboat without having a laugh at the expense of Gilmour, who is a great friend of mine. Next to the pretty girl the most distracting influence on the island is the cow. There is only one cow, and I generally make a remark to it as I go past. It pays no attention; but that I do not greatly mind. I have studied the cow until I fancy I know more about it than most people. If it was the cow I wanted to think of instead of my hero, I fancy I could do it. There are also sad-looking men who bring fishing rods and stools to the island. They sit all on the stools, and pit themselves against a large-sized minnow, which one of them catches perhaps twice a week. Then the curious ones lay down their rods, and gathering round the minnow, watch it slowly dying on the grass. The jealous ones pretend not to notice, and however loud the successful angler may shout in his triumph, they never turn their heads. When I ought to be going round thinking I frequently find myself lying on the sward talking to the fishers. They are like myself in this respect – that they are all more hopeful than the circumstances seem to warrant'.

*Walker London*, a title which recalls a Victorian catch-phrase, was at first called *The Houseboat*, but had to be changed when the play had its première in the West End, as it was found that there was another which already had that title. It showed Barrie's obvious talents for stagecraft, and ran over 500 performances, a foretaste of his long line of box office successes. The stage directions for the first act set the scene: 'A houseboat on the Thames. Curtain rises on houseboat, blinds down. Time: morning. A canoe and punt, on bank at bow, tied to houseboat. Someone in the distance is playing a penny whistle. W.G. is lying on a plank, lazily writing a letter. Presently he sleeps. Nanny on deck fishing'. Like *When a Man's Single*, it tells the story of a rather ordinary young man with grand illusions who gatecrashes higher society, indulging itself on the houseboat at Tagg's Island, where the normal conventions were slightly relaxed, but pushes off rapidly when his real status is about to be found out.

After that first season Barrie gave up the houseboat, but he never forgot his rapturous days on the island, even though he did not visit Tagg's again for another thirty years. In 1919 he came back to dine, not in the hotel he had known, but in a grander affair. He was now famous, a household name. What memories must have crowded in as he looked again at the haunts of the struggling young journalist. He recalls them all – the houseboats – the small hotel – even Tagg's solitary cow – in a little memoir published in the 1920s thinly disguising himself as 'James Anon': 'I visited the scene lately and found it was now as grand as if it were being presented nightly at Drury Lane. There remained no houseboats of our humble kind; magnificent successors encircled Tagg's Island. Each seems to have a garden; there is a gorgeous hotel, and there are putting-greens and lawn-tennis courts and dancing galore. I was discomforted, because I had thought it a gay place in my day and that I had been seeing life. Now I know that by comparison we were all humdrum folk, living prosaically round a field with a cow in it, a cow that became the one companion of Anon. There was a little inn with a bar, where he sometimes went forlornly to listen to the swashbucklers from the other houseboats. Mr Anon thought that anybody in flannels was a swashbuckler. On the island in the heat of the day Anon and the cow often had the field to themselves, for the flannelled ones were at their offices in the city, and we are speaking of an age when women did not want to bask and be brown. The cow browsed, and Anon meditated'.

In 1889 Tom Tagg reached his fiftieth birthday, which he celebrated by announcing that he was branching out into yet another business venture. He had leased about three acres of land opposite the island on the Molesey shore, on which it was his intention to erect a boat club-house, a structure which would have a large boathouse at the ground level, above which would be club premises, with lounges, dining rooms, etc, and bedrooms over the top. Patrons would pay a yearly subscription to belong to the club, and would be able to come down, stay the week-end, hire a boat, play games like tennis or billiards, dine, or dance, all in the same establishment. 'The plans of the building', it was reported, 'have been approved of, and tenders are already being sought for carrying out the work. The structure will have a frontage of eighty feet, standing back forty feet from the towpath. It will be constructed of red brick, and of Gothic-Dutch architecture'. The architect was Mr A. Burrell-Burrell, of Chancery Lane.

The building was commenced soon afterwards and was constructed by a local builder, Mr E. Potterton of East Molesey. It was fitted throughout with all the latest innovations – electric light, telephone and electric bells.

It was formally opened on 2 May 1891. The *Surrey Comet* reported the event: 'Thanks to the enterprise of Messrs. T.G. Tagg and Son the neighbourhood is now in possession of one of the most picturesque-looking and perfectly equipped riverside club-houses in the kingdom. The building itself commands a view over one of the most delightful reaches of the Thames – from the Water Gallery to Garrick's Temple – The base of the building is occupied as a boat-house, and a highly attractive one it is likely to prove; the spacious grounds adjoining are tastefully laid out, and there are capital facilities for the enjoyment of lawn tennis bowling and quoits. The annual subscription at present is two guineas for home and one guinea for foreign and colonial; but we understand that fees will shortly be raised. The club premises comprise: On the first floor (a) A magnificent club-room, 60 ft × 30ft with parquet floor, capable of dining upwards of 300 people at one time. It is also eminently adapted for ball-room or smoking concerts. (b) A very fine reading room 30ft × 15ft. (c) Two fine billiard rooms. (d) A ladies drawing room. (e) A private dining room, for parties not exceeding 20. (f) A members lavatory. (g) A secretary's room, refreshment bar, etc. On the second floor (a) Six large bedrooms, for the use of members only, with balcony commanding views of the river and Hurst Park racecourse. (b) Bathroom and lavatory with hot and cold water, kitchen, etc. The formal opening took place on Saturday evening last, when, despite the unpropitious weather, about sixty members and friends assembled to partake of the banquet provided'. The magnificent parquet floor was composed of over 8,000 pieces of selected woods of 'every variety of grain and hue'.

In June 1897, on the hot sultry day of Queen Victoria's Diamond Jubilee, Tom Tagg caught a cold, from which he died three days later. He was only 57. As a result the firm was taken over by his son George John Tagg, remembered by many Molesey people as 'Colonel Tagg', who had been taken on as a partner in the firm several years before. He was described in 1899 as 'a gentleman of considerable classical culture, and knowledge of belles lettres'. He had been educated at Hampton Grammar School and in France, before being trained as a marine engineer in which capacity he designed most of the launches built by the firm. During the First World War, because of his knowledge of the Continental waterways, and of boats and boating in general, he was appointed as Assistant Director of Inland Water Transport in France and Belgium and Liaison Officer with the allied armies and navies, with the rank of Lt Col. For his work in this respect he was twice mentioned in dispatches and was awarded the OBE and the French Croix de Guerre. In the Second War he joined the Civil Defence, and in his black beret was a familiar figure around Molesey.

However George Tagg was not the stubborn business type his father was. For a few years very little changed, and then, probably due to the effects of the Boer War, the advent of the motor car, and the changing social climate, high society and the better-off moved away from the river. Trade fell away, there were a number of poor seasons (it must be remembered that bad weather hits the riverside, and especially an island venture, much more heavily than most), and Tagg found himself in financial difficulties. To ease matters the hotel was taken over in May 1903 by a limited company, of which Tagg was one of the chief shareholders, but matters became worse and in the following year he was declared bankrupt, with liabilities amounting to £6,906.

In December 1904 all his assets were put up for auction, including the lease of the hotel, five and a half acres of ground on the island, and the boat-building premises, £850 worth of shares in Taggs Island Hotel Ltd, the freehold of the club and boathouse on the Molesey bank of the river, and the land between the club and the lock-house. The fleet of steam and motor launches, boats, skiffs, punts, and canoes, together with the plant and machinery and flags and bunting were also auctioned, as were the furniture and effects. The auction drew a large crowd of people, especially of boating and river men, 'many of whom', it was said, 'had no doubt spent many happy hours about the place', but apparently the bids did not flow as freely as the nostalgia, and a number of lots were withdrawn when the reserve price was not reached.

The club and boat-house was one of the lots not sold. Eventually it was taken over by a group of mainly local people whose members ran it under the name of 'The New Hampton Court Club'. After renovations and re-furnishing it was opened on 16 July 1906. The *Surrey Comet* prophesied: 'No doubt the club will supply a want'. This, in fact, it did until the 1920s, when the premises were eventually taken over by Watercraft Ltd, who used them for the manufacture of lifeboats and other sea-worthy motor boats, and was one of the first firms to use fibre-glass extensively for the construction of this type of craft. After a long period of successful boat-building here, offering employment to a number of local men, Watercraft closed down a few years ago and the site is now divided into factories, whose future at the moment seems uncertain. Nevertheless the building still nobly displays a plaque with the monogram 'TGT & Son', in proud memory of the magnificent splendour with which its life began, but which it was not for long able to sustain.

Meanwhile the hotel was still being run by 'Tagg's Island Hotel Ltd', but apparently without a great deal of success. In 1908 John Bradford, of the luxury houseboat *Gipsy*, wrote a letter to F.J. Kent, the owner of the island freehold, complaining about the bad state and decay of the island in general but of the hotel in particular. He suggested that a syndicate of business men should be set up to inject fresh capital into the place and to take over the running, stating that if this did not happen 'the better class of trade will be killed'. Several abortive attempts were tried to float such a company, but without success. Tagg's original lease was due to run out at the end of 1911, and it was imperative that a working solution be found as quickly as possible. The only practical proposition which stood any chance of success, and the one which was eventually adopted, involved another houseboat owner – Fred Westcott.

ABOVE: Mr H. Herwitt's magnificent houseboat, *Satsuma*, (reproduced from *Victorians on the Thames* by R.R. Bolland, published by Evans Brothers Ltd.) BELOW: Platts Ait seen from West Molesey, when the Immisch Electric Launch Co Ltd boasted 'Royal patronage' and did everything, from building to hiring, and from housing to mending steam, electric and oil-driven launches.

The Late TOM TAGG,
Pioneer of high-class Launches
and Boats on Upper Thames.

Founder of Tagg's Island.

BY ROYAL WARRANT TO THEIR MAJESTIES
The Late QUEEN VICTORIA and The Late KING EDWARD VII.

TWELVE GOLD & PRIZE MEDALS AWARDED.

## TOM TAGG & SON,

Above the Lock, HAMPTON COURT.

No connection with any other firm of the same name in the immediate neighbourhood.

## TOM TAGG & SON, Tagg's Island, HAMPTON COURT.

*present respectful compliments to their numerous Royal and influential patrons and customers in all parts of the World and take this opportunity of tendering thanks for past and continued favors accorded them.*

*They desire to state for general information, that the Business will still be carried on under personal supervision of Mr. GEORGE J. TAGG, M.Inst., N.A., past Vice-President and one of the Founders of the Thames Boat Builders Association.*

*Special attention is called to the fact that this business is not connected with any other Boating Business in the neighbourhood, and that, to avoid delays, all correspondence should be fully addressed as directed herein.*

*TAGG'S ISLAND is universally known, and with its recent improvements and modern attractions is now one of the greatest River Resorts in the World.*

*All visitors to London should include Tagg's Island in their pleasureable arrangements.*

ABOVE: The Tagg dynasty carries on. (A note on the front of this brochure laconically remarks 'Left Island 1913 for good'.) OPPOSITE ABOVE: The *Gypsy* houseboat at Tagg's Island; LEFT: the Swiss Chalet is now part of a boat building yard. RIGHT: the *River Dream* with *Gypsy* beyond. BELOW: 'Many people not only frequent the river in their spare time, but even live on it in houseboats...' says the legend on this painting of exotic weekend floating retreats at Tagg's Island early this century.

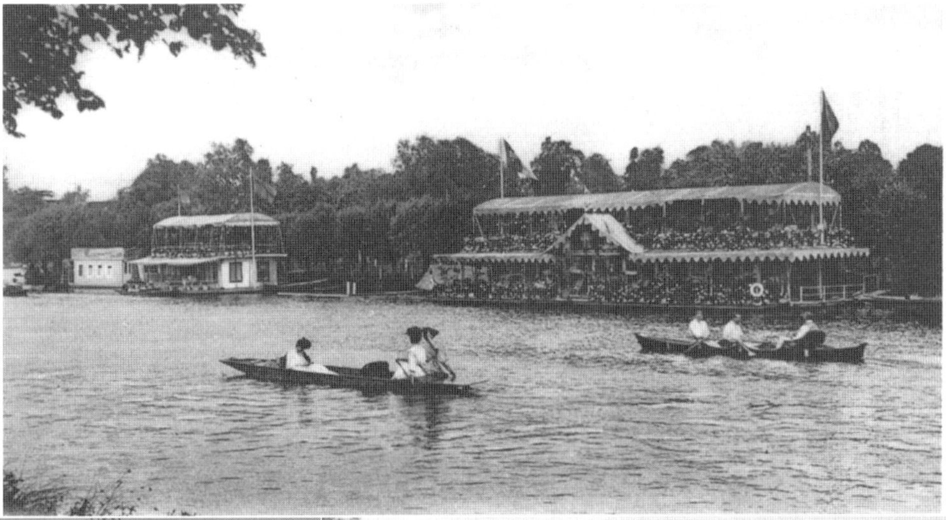

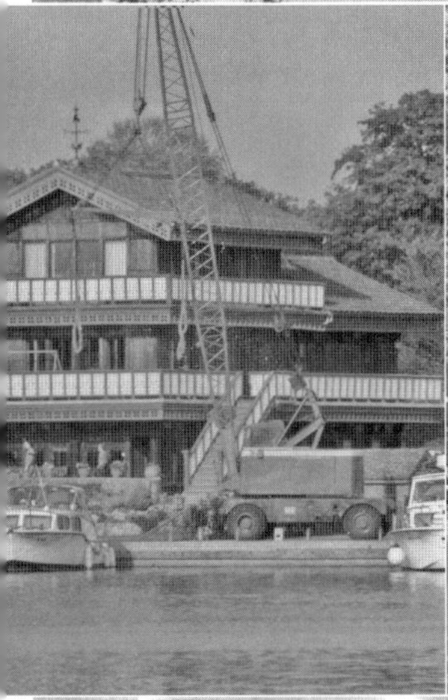

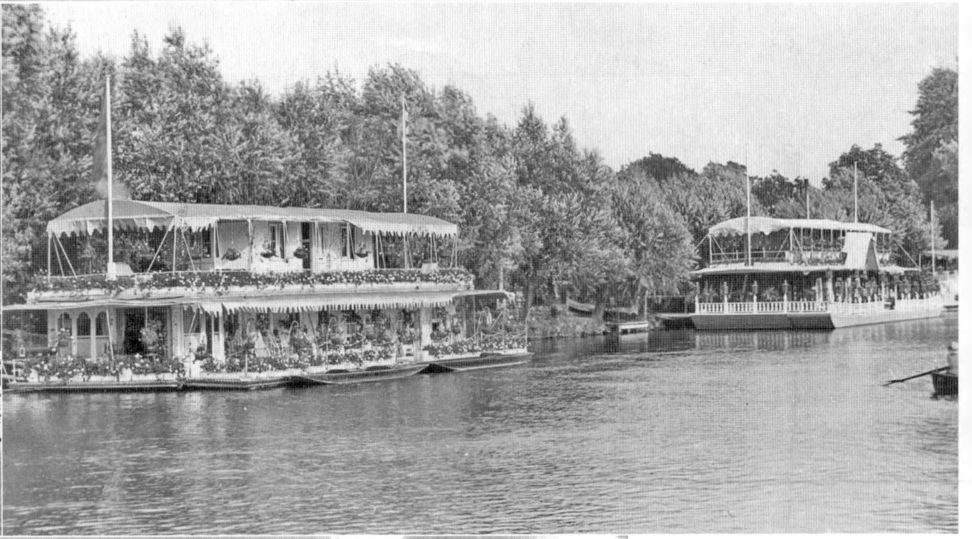

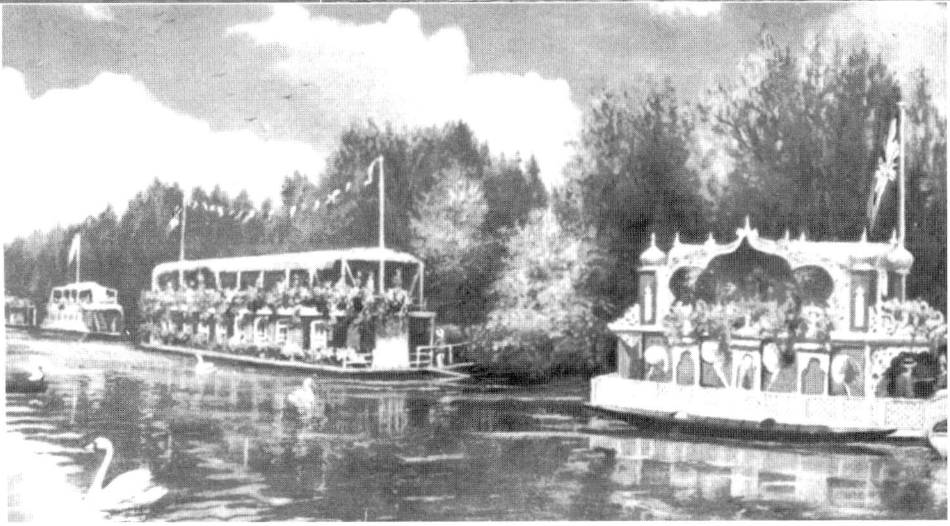

ABOVE: The houseboats with their lanterns are a magnet for lesser vessels, as Edwardian Londoners relax. BELOW: The Island and Hotel in 1901. OPPOSITE: It was all up for grabs on 1 December 1904.

BY ORDER OF THE TRUSTEE.

# HAMPTON COURT.

## The Particulars and Conditions of Sale

OF THE

VALUABLE MODERN AND SUBSTANTIALLY-BUILT

# FREEHOLD PREMISES

KNOWN AS

### "The Hampton Court Club" & "Tagg's Boat House,"

Also the Exceptionally Desirable and World-wide Renowned

## LEASEHOLD RIVER PROPERTY

KNOWN AS

### Tagg's Island, East Molesey,

With the Substantially-built

## FULLY-LICENSED HOTEL

(Which is underlet to Tagg's Island Hotel, Limited),

HAVING

### Boat Houses and Outbuildings,

AND

## GROUNDS OF ABOUT 5½ ACRES.

ALSO

### 850 £1 SHARES IN TAGG'S ISLAND HOTEL, LTD.

Which will be Sold by Auction by Messrs.

# HERRING, SON & DAW

Upon the Premises, "HAMPTON COURT CLUB," EAST MOLESEY,

### On THURSDAY, 1st DECEMBER, 1904

At TWELVE o'clock precisely, IN LOTS.

The Properties may be Viewed by Orders to be obtained of Messrs. HERRING, SON & DAW. Particulars with Conditions of Sale may be had at Tagg's Island Hotel; of

**Messrs. GADSDEN & TREHERNE**, Solicitors, 28, Bedford Row, W.C.;
**Messrs. GANE, JACKSON, JEFFERYS, WELLS & Co.**, Chartered Accountants, 66, Coleman Street, E.C.; and of
**Messrs. HERRING, SON & DAW**, Auctioneers,
6, IRONMONGER LANE, CHEAPSIDE, E.C., and 312, BRIXTON HILL, S.W.

*Telephones: 5964 Bank; 130 Streatham.*

ABOVE: The ladies board a launch at Barge Walk in 1905. LEFT: Tom Tagg's Boat Clubhouse was eventually taken over by Watercraft Ltd. RIGHT: His monogram is on the wall of the building.

# Fred Westcott

Fred John Westcott was born in the city of Exeter in 1866, the son of working class people. Whilst still almost a child he was sent to work for a plumber, but his heart was not in it; he dreamt all day long of becoming an entertainer. Every penny he earned and every spare moment he could squeeze was spent in training to become an acrobat. Eventually he considered he was proficient enough and trudged to London where he managed to secure some bookings in the music halls. In between engagements, he and other performers took to busking on the London streets, and on sunny week-ends they brought their acts – singing, playing and acrobatics – down to Molesey. This was the part that Fred liked most; here was life, colour and gaiety. Here, too, he looked across the water and saw the pampered upper crust luxuriating on their magnificent houseboats, and made a devout pledge: 'One day I too will be rich, and one of the first things I'll do will be to have a houseboat on Tagg's Island'.

His favourite spot was Molesey Lock for, when the boats were locked in the basin, he had a captive audience. He performed his little act and then thrust a net down to all the vessels – large and small, punts and launches alike – and in went the money.

Westcott had an innate business sense and took every opportunity to fulfil his ambition. He worked ceaselessly, he saved, he scraped; at this time in his life he became notably parsimonious (an attitude which was to change dramatically). Perhaps the turning point came when a troupe known as The Three Karnos, who should have been performing at the same theatre, failed to turn up. The energetic Fred, who had watched the act many times and espied the chance of making a little extra cash, persuaded two of his colleagues to join with him, dress up, and do the act in their stead, as well as their own. They did it with so much success that they were kept on, and eventually Fred adopted the act as his own – Fred Westcott became Fred Karno – a name which was to ring around the world as synonymous with knockabout comedy, fun, and laughter.

Karno was to make his name and fortune, however, not by his own stage performance but by the antics of others. He started his own troupe and began putting on his own shows. Here his natural astuteness really began to show. His perception of the potential talent of other artists was uncanny. The shows he put on became better and better, and moved higher and higher. His 'fun factory', as it was known, produced such well-known spectacles as 'Mumming Birds', 'Jail Birds', 'Fred Karno's Army', and many others, and put many a comedian on the road to stardom. The list of recruits who owed their later success to starting out under the Karno banner is extensive, starting off with the daddy of them all –the incomparable Charlie Chaplin – but including such other greats as: Stan Laurel, Will Hay, Fred Kitchin, Billy Bennett, Max Miller, Sid Walker, Sandy Powell, Bobby Howes, Gene Gerrard, Robb Wilton, Syd Chaplin, Barry Lupino, Flanagan and Allen, Nervo and Knox, Naughton and Gold, and so many others. It seems as if Karno's judgment on a completely unknown artist's capabilities was never wrong, and he would travel miles to witness the performance of some struggling entertainer with the makings of a topliner, but would never engage anybody whom he was not convinced could make the grade. Much of the fortune he consequentially made was undoubtedly due to his practice of employing unknown talent at cheap rates and training them himself, rather than paying tip-top wages to some well-known and well-established name. To all the people who worked for him, from the stars down to stage hands and carpenters he was known simply as 'The Guvnor'.

True to the vow he had made whilst an unknown towpath busker, one of the first things he did when money began to flow was to acquire a houseboat on Tagg's Island. This was in 1903 and the houseboat was called *Highland Lassie*. From then on Fred spent as much time as he could on his new purchase. He had always been regarded as something of a womaniser, and the houseboat developed into an ideally sequestered love-nest – an early version of what became known as the casting couch. Even his son, Fred Karno junior, was 'quite awed by the procession of girls – by no means all of them actresses – who moved through my father's cabin next door to me', and he had to be bribed to keep the knowledge of this veritable floating harem secret, not only from his mother, but also from his father's 'official' mistress.

The houseboat became, not only a free and easy river retreat, wherein he could forget the cares of his 'fun factory', but also a place where he could throw parties to impress his theatrical friends and assist his rise up the social ladder. For the working lad who had started out as a fairground acrobat and towpath busker was now mixing with the swells – and loving every minute of it. Fred was swayed by the society in which he now found himself; they accepted him because he was probably far richer than most of them would ever be, and because this caterer of entertainment for the masses was one of the most popular and well-known men in Britain.

The fortune he had scraped and saved he was now ready to spend – and spend lavishly. The skinflint now became the spendthrift. The *Highland Lassie*, although grand and comfortable in its way, was not grand enough. He had to have something far more magnificent. He had to be the owner of the biggest and most luxurious houseboat on the river. Like all his theatrical ventures it had to be the most spectacular production ever.

Once fixed on the idea he set to work with his usual enthusiasm and earnestness. The layout he devised himself, with the help and advice of anybody he could find, including Mr Henry Hewitt, who had built himself what was then thought of as the finest houseboat on the Thames – *Satsuma* – which was moored at Platts Ait just up the river. After spending much time discussing the plans, he had his chief stage carpenter make a wooden scale model, perfect in every detail, to see what it would look like and to reassure himself for he was going to expend a great deal of money. The hull was laid down at Brentford and, after launching, it was towed up to Tagg's Island, ready to receive the superstructure and living quarters. Everything was absolutely de luxe, the most expensive, the most lavish. The spacious saloon and the cabins were all panelled in solid mahogany, the floors were thickly carpeted, the window frames were bronze, and the bathroom was walled and fitted with washbasins, all in finest marble. Electric light, water, and the telephone were installed and the rich furnishings were supplied by Maples of Tottenham Court Road. The sun deck, ninety feet long by eighteen feet wide, was surmounted by an elaborate wrought-iron framework, over which could be drawn a canvas awning, and on which hundreds of electric fairy lamps were suspended to flood it with light for evening dances, for these a full orchestra was often engaged. It was the nonparcil of houseboats, even larger and more luxurious than *Satsuma*; all others paled to mere floating camps beside it. This vast wonder, which was christened *Astoria*, cost a sum variously estimated up to £20,000, an enormous amount in 1913.

When it was all finished, Fred had to have an opening night dinner, a sort of grand première; over a hundred guests were present. Joe Lyons was hired to do the catering, at a cost of nearly two pounds a head, not including drinks. After dinner there was music and dancing on the upper deck, for those who received no invitation there was always the river and the towpath from which to gape at those who had. Around the animated houseboat it was said so many little boats were packed that it was possible to step from one to the other from the Molesey bank right across to Hampton.

Karno's houseboat was moored close to another, called *Cosy Corner*, occupied by Henry A. Lytton, a well-known Gilbert and Sullivan opera singer, and a close friendship developed between the two.

With England's most successful showman and England's most popular Savoyard both in residence, it was not long before their neighbours and other Thames devotees began pestering them to use their influence to bolster up the attractions of the island. Not that Fred required much pressing on that score. He fairly lapped up the publicity that serving on committees and organising charity shows brought. During the summer of 1907, for instance, the two organised a great water carnival, under the magnificent title 'The Grand Fete des Theatres'.

These *divertissements* brought a number of people to the island and custom to the hotel, but were only held occasionally. At other times the paucity of patrons was obvious. It became increasingly evident that what was required was a new and vigorous management and a generous transfusion of fresh capital. Where, however, were these desiderata to be found? Karno, as everyone now knew, possessed organising ability, business acumen, contacts in the world of entertainment, an enthusiastic nature and, most important of all, a considerable fortune to boot, which he was now eager to spend. Who better to take over the place? He was approached and, after much discussion and persuasion, he agreed to do so. The houseboat owners feared that, if the hotel failed, the island would be sold for building development and their mooring leases would not be renewed. An agreement was drawn up and Karno took over the island for a term of forty-two years from Christmas 1912.

*Astoria* takes shape on Tagg's Island in 1911.

ABOVE: *Astoria* at Tagg's Island. BELOW: Mr and Mrs Fred Karno take their ease aboard *Astoria* on 28 June 1913.

# KARSINO

On 7 October *The Times* announced: 'Mr. Fred Karno, the music-hall artist, who for some years had a houseboat moored to Tagg's Island, East Molesey, has arranged to take over the island. He proposes to run free ferries to it from the shore, and to provide entertainments and illuminations in the evening'. It is perhaps with thoughts in mind of the type of entertainment that Karno might provide if left to his own devices, that the owners, still the Kent family, wrote a clause into the lease specifically prohibiting any 'theatre, music-hall, swing, roundabout, switchback, railway, toboggan run, cocoa nut shy, or any other such erection' on the island. Neither was there to be any advertising. We can visualise his rather more aristocratic neighbours insisting on these stipulations. They wanted an increase in the number of people using the hotel, but what they did not want was Southend or Blackpool transferred to Molesey on Thames. It was to be very discreet and very middle class.

In spite of the enthusiasm with which Fred Karno took up his new venture, he must soon have had misgivings. He poured money into it, but even he had no bottomless purse. On 5 November, after he had just learned that yet more expense would be incurred in bringing the sewerage across the river, we find him writing to C.W. Kent, 'I am just beginning to realise the enormous magnitude of the task I have undertaken with regard to the island... I fear it will not be a profitable investment by any means'. If only he could have realised how prophetic his words were to prove!

The first thing was to rebuild the hotel and, as it was still nominally under the control of Mr George Tagg at least until Christmas 1912, he presented plans to the magistrates for approval, saying that the then premises were somewhat out of date. Consent was, therefore, given for 'important alterations and improvements', the contemplated outlay for which was estimated at about £7,000. Before long the site was given over to an army of workmen, who did somewhat more than 'alterations and improvements'. The old building was, in fact, completely demolished and a magnificent new one started to rise in its place. In the true Karno style of having nothing but the biggest and best in everything, it had to be much larger, much grander, and much more up to date than its predecessor, with every known innovation. Instead of the paltry £7,000 suggested to the sessions, the eventual bill for the hotel alone was something like £40,000.

As architect for the new hotel, Karno employed Frank Matcham, perhaps the most outstanding exponent of 'theatrical baroque', which reached its zenith in the Edwardian era. Matcham's commissions include such masterpieces as the London Hippodrome (now the Talk of the Town), the London Coliseum, the Empire Cinema in Leicester Square, the Victoria Palace and Richmond Theatre. All of these are ornate, flamboyant, and rococo, but show a genuine love of the theatre, a sort of playhouse panache. In designing the Island Hotel, however, Matcham was much more constrained, and thereby showed his genius, for the building he produced, although ornamental, was neither gaudy nor over-decorated. It mingled unobtrusively with its delightful backcloth of trees and river.

Even its construction was novel. The site, being confined and water-logged, required a new approach. Many tons of concrete had to be poured into the foundations and, to make the structure light but strong, the large building was fabricated from a steel framework with walls of concrete slabs, one of the first buildings in this country to be so erected, and so revolutionary that no such construction was catered for in the local building bye-laws, which had to be specially amended to permit its being built at all. This held up operations for a time, but the plans were finally passed at a meeting of the Hampton UDC on Tuesday 14 January 1913, and work commenced right away.

In a newspaper interview Karno claimed that the new hotel would be 'a sumptuous place, with all the comforts of home and a good many more too'; it would be 'the finest and most luxurious river hotel in Europe' and 'there is going to be nothing vulgar about the place', he added; 'we are doing our best to keep the place refined'.

The demise of the old hotel, however, was something not entirely applauded by everyone. The *Surrey Comet*, for instance, said 'the passing of the old Tagg's Island, with its modest charming appearance, is in some senses to be deplored'. They balanced this by noting 'the handsome appearance of the grand new hotel'.

The 'Karsino', as the new hotel was christened, had a double verandah on three sides, on which visitors could take lunch, tea or dinner, or just lounge and admire the scenery. It also boasted twenty-six bedrooms, each with hot and cold running water, and each commanding its own view of the river. There were lifts to all floors, and electric lights were fitted throughout. Fred's policy of being first and foremost in everything is even reflected in the telephone – its number was Molesey 1. The telephone was the cause of some excitement soon after the hotel opened; the wires across to the mainland were struck by lightning, and three men working underneath were slightly dazed, though not hurt. The commotion of the affair, however, was too much for one of the lady guests – she promptly fainted.

The *pièce-de-résistance* of the hotel was the Palm Court. It was large enough to seat some eight hundred people, with a maple dancing floor, under an extensive dome, and with the ceiling painted with a number of scenes of the river between Hampton Court and Windsor. It was truly a magnificent ballroom. Even thirty years later, when the present writer used to dance there with the lady who was to become his wife, it still retained a noble atmosphere – or was it because we were young and so full of romance? The stage was cunningly constructed with two prosceniums, one facing into the ballroom, the other at the back, facing the lawn outside. As Karno himself explained: 'In cold or wet weather we shall give concerts and entertainments in the Palm Court, and in fine weather the same stage will be used, but the audience will sit outside on the lawn. You see, if it rains, all we have to do is to fetch the audience inside, draw up one backcloth and lower the other, turn the artists round, and get on with the show'.

The concerts were given twice daily throughout the season by some of the leading entertainers, orchestras and military bands of the day. The prices of admission were something which will surely bring torrents of nostalgia flooding back to those who can remember such days – 6d, 1s and 2s.

There was also a resident orchestra, and here again Karno showed his inborn genius for discovering unknown talent; he employed as leader a young musician named Jack Hylton, who was to become a household name, leader of his own dance band, one of the most popular in the inter-war years, and eventually a theatrical impresario almost as well-known as Karno himself.

The hotel, however, was not the only attraction of Karsino. The whole island was now given over to diversions for its patrons. The grounds were laid out in a lavish scale by one of the most eminent landscape gardeners. There was a lawn over six hundred feet long, with various walks and terraces 'arranged in floral profusion', and a pergola which stretched right athwart the island, with a bandstand in the middle. There was a Dutch garden and a German beer garden. 'I have' said Mr Karno 'tried my best to bring the Continental atmosphere up-river'. There were tennis, croquet, bowls and badminton courts, and a 'quaintly-pretty' new boat-house, from which visitors could hire boats or launches, and moor their own boats while dining in the restaurant or patronising the theatre. 'At each up-river corner of the boat-house two artistic little kiosks face the Molesey and Hampton sides of the stream', said a contemporary description, 'one of which is the office of the Karsino manager, Mr John Daly'.

As Karsino had no direct communication with the mainland, all visitors had to be ferried over, and for this purpose there was a fleet of 'large and artistic' punts, commuting between the island and both banks, and a landing stage was constructed near the end of what is now called 'Graburn Way'. A most modern innovation, considering that this was 1913, was that on both sides there was a larger punt for ferrying over guests' motor cars, and a garage capable of accommodating forty cars was erected on the island, where petrol and accessories could be obtained and repairs carried out. At first all the ferries were free but, in order to keep down the thousands of sightseers who just came over to stare or to wander around the grounds without spending any money, Karno instituted a system whereby patrons were charged a shilling to be ferried over, deducted from the bill when paid.

At dusk during the season Karsino probably looked its finest. All the grounds and terraces were illuminated 'with myriads of coloured electric lights in the foliage' which, together with the Chinese lanterns and glittering facades of the houseboats still ringing the island, must have appeared a veritable fairyland. Even Karno himself said it was to be 'regarded as something unique'. And to add to the enchantment, a large captive balloon, with the letters KARSINO painted on the sides, was flown above, whilst a searchlight positioned on the roof of the hotel focussed a stream of light upon it.

No expense was spared in advertising the venture, and luring patrons to the island. All the latest innovations were pressed into service. The people of London looked up into the sky amazed as an aeroplane circled above them, trailing behind it a huge streamer announcing its attractions.

Karno said 'I have put up a splendid affair, I shall revive the glories of fetes such as Vauxhall saw in its palmiest days, a glittering palace of delight, the most beautiful pleasure resort on the Thames'. This palace of delight was opened on Sunday 22 June 1913. At the celebration lunch party Sir Thomas Dewar of the whisky distilling family, later Lord Dewar, proposed a toast of 'success to the Karsino and the new Island Hotel'. He said that he hoped sincerely that Mr Karno's venture would be crowned with success. The Karsino was just such a place as London wanted, and it would no doubt become a distinct feature in its social life.

The Karno publicity machine went to work with a will, plastering the whole metropolis with posters, so that no Londoner was left in any doubt as to what was taking place on Tagg's island in the glorious river Thames. It was confidently expected that some hundreds would turn up, and a suitable store of food and drink was got in to cater for them. In the event many thousands packed onto the island. At one time it was almost impossible to move. The ferry boats, which were operated for the day by a bevy of beautiful actresses, wearing dresses of white and Wedgwood blue, had to stop conveying any more people across, and so many thousands were left to line the banks on either side of the river, most of whom never did get into Karsino. Those who did found that the catering department had gone haywire trying to provide for such a vast unexpected crowd. Never in his wildest dreams did Karno expect such a turn-out, and very soon the food ran out. Men were sent out to scour the district, knocking up tradesmen from their Sunday rest, and rushing back with whatever they could muster. By evening not a morsel was to be had for miles around. Karno had chosen a Sunday for the opening so that all his performers could come along and lend a hand; they were quickly pressed into service. Actresses went into the kitchens and prepared food. Knockabout comedians served as waiters. By some miracle it all seemed to come right. It looked as if Karsino was definitely set on a prosperous course.

For a time it seemed successful enough. On a fine summer Sunday the swells would come down from London, the river was packed with flannelled and boatered young men and parasolled young ladies, and the tills might ring up a four-figure sum. There was also a regular clientele from the social set – royalty, politicians, businessmen, and the like.

Unfortunately, soon after Karsino opened its doors, the sunshine of success was overcast by the gathering clouds of world war. Some of its best customers were Continentals, mostly German and French, and those quickly vanished; for a while the prospect looked bleak. However, the very darkness of the time helped. It became a little oasis of glamour and gaiety amid the sombre reality of war and sorrow. Young servicemen home on leave from the front brought their wives and sweethearts for a last wild spree before returning to an uncertain fate. And when Hurst Park racecourse became a training airfield for the Royal Flying Corps, the numbers increased. Even those poor lads who changed their battle khaki for hospital blue found refuge on the island, as they were invited to parties by various organisations. In May 1917, although the war had been grinding on for almost three years, the *Surrey Comet* reported that 'Arrangements for the river season at the Karsino on Tagg's Island are now almost completed, and everything points to a successful summer term notwithstanding the serious handicap due to the war. The Karsino has become a very popular venue for entertaining wounded soldiers and numerous parties of men from London and other places have recently enjoyed the quiet and seclusion of the island'.

As soon as peace was declared, however, the glitter and tinsel began to tarnish. Karno opened up again with enthusiasm, expecting the same patrons as before the war, but enthusiasm was not enough. The boom had gone. Public taste had changed. Things were more sophisticated, and most of all the motor car was here to stay. The river was losing its pull. There is no doubt, in spite of Karno's advertisement of 'popular prices', that Karsino was expensive, its clients had been socialites of the upper and upper-middle classes, the sort of people who now sought their pleasures further afield.

Karno had sunk some £70,000 in the venture, perhaps a million pounds in modern terms, but the money so liberally spent was not backed by receipts at the cash desk. The entertainment trade has known many grand enterprises, and there are few other business pursuits in which the capital is gobbled up so quickly and the returns so hazardous. In addition, an undertaking centred on an island, relying on river trade, is of course most susceptible to the vagaries of the English climate. The season is in any case a short one; just one poor year could be calamity and several in succession were indeed a catastrophe.

Nevertheless, Karno struggled on, hoping that fortune would change, but in 1926 the creditors started knocking on the door, and the man who had brought the music-hall to millions was forced to face the music himself. To stave them off, he started selling his assets, *Astoria* went for a mere fraction of its original cost. All this coincided with the slump in the music-hall, hit by the growth of cinema and wireless, a blow from which it never recovered. Had it not been so, Fred might have been able to carry on. As it was, everything seemed to conspire to go awry at the same time, and the strain was too much for his resources.

In April 1926 he sold the tenancy rights for three years, with an option to purchase at the end of the term, to the New Princes Restaurant of Picadilly, for £2,500. This, however, was not enough to satisfy his debts, a judgement for £6,000 was levied against his goods and chattels on the island, and eventually the mortgagees took over Karsino entirely. Fred was finally declared bankrupt in the autumn of 1927, and it is rather ironical, in view of the large sums involved, that the order against him was for the relatively paltry amount of £141, the outstanding debt on a loan of £200 he had obtained from a moneylender, which he was unable to repay, although it was reported that there were some forty other actions pending against the estate. At his examination, Karno attributed his troubles entirely to having been persuaded to take over Tagg's Island, assessing his losses on the venture at about £100,000. Soon afterwards he retired to the West Country. He took a wine shop at Poole in Dorset, where he died on 17 September 1941, leaving £42 7s 4d.

Some people have tried to blame Karno's losses entirely on wet weather, but the years 1920 to 1924 were in fact some of the finest on record. Indeed, 1921 was the driest year in over a century of meteorological recording, and one of the sunniest too. His fault seems really to lie in that he failed to perceive the changed circumstances which ruled in post-war times. He sighed nostalgically for his former clients and to keep the place 'refined'. Unfortunately the 'refined' of the 1920s no longer wished to patronise the island. Edwardian upper crust gaiety had become one of the casualties of the war, and the slump which followed did nothing to revive it. Had Fred recognised this trend and cast his net wider, Karsino might have been with us yet.

When the New Princes' Restaurant took over from Fred Karno, its Managing Director was a Mr Beaumont Alexander, a young man full of new ideas and full of new enthusiasm. Undaunted by Karno's recent experience, the company plunged straight in with a scheme of expansion which promised 'scenes of festivity on a scale never witnessed before, not even under Mr Karno'. Their intention was to convert this island into a miniature Palm Beach, Or, as Mr Alexander explained, 'a resemblance of America's most exclusive resort in Florida, thousands of tons of sand are to be placed on the island and hundreds of palms will be planted. There will be large sunshades, beach chairs, provision for the enjoyment of mixed bathing, and other items of amusement and relaxation generally associated with the fashionable resorts. A fleet of motor-boats, punts and canoes will be provided for river merrymakers'. He went on: 'We have not in London an original road house, such as are to be found in the neighbourhood of Paris and the principal centres throughout America, and we intend to make the Karsino a rendezvous of that description'.

A grand opening gala was held on 8 May 1926, when Jack Smith, known as 'the whispering baritone', one of the idols of the day, was engaged as the star attraction, to back up the resident cabaret company, 'the New Princes' Frivolities', and Alfredo and his band, later a well-known broadcaster.

It was a doughty start to a doughty project, but again still not enough to ensure its success. In less than two years Mr Alexander and the New Princes' were broken.

In April 1928, when it was obvious that the Palm Beach venture was going to fold, Charles Pearce-Brown, who had been an assistant manager, borrowed enough money to persuade the leaseholder to convey the island to him. Pearce-Brown was one of those interesting characters who have tried many things in their life. He started in musical comedy and vaudeville with a touring company, which eventually went to America. We next find him as a salesman for various companies, selling all sorts of things from oil to steel wire, and as a professional heavy-weight boxer being groomed as the 'White hope' to meet Jack Johnson. In 1913 he began to deal in shares on the New York Stock Exchange, but he crashed in 1915, due (he said) to the sinking of the *Lusitania,* and he was then employed by the US Shipping Board on war work. After the war he returned to this country and became interested in theatrical advertising; he started up a business under the name Herbert Cyril & Co. In conjunction with some others he opened the Embassy Theatre in Oxford Street –

which was a financial flop; in 1925 he branched out as an impresario, assisting in the production of revues – which were also financial flops. So he came to be on Tagg's Island using the name Herbert Cyril.

Once more the same procedure was gone through, and a considerable slice of the borrowed money was expended on improvements. Mr Alexander's theme had been an American Palm Beach; Mr Cyril's was to be a Continental Riviera. Again there was a total transformation and, to perfect the theme, the name was also changed. No longer was it to be the ill-fated 'Karsino', now it was to be the 'Thames Riviera'. In order to open in time for the summer season, within nine weeks there had been built a completely covered tennis court with a battery of arc lamps producing artificial sunlight to enable it to be used day and night, and a magnificent skating rink with a then brand new process of producing ice chemically, of which Mr Cyril held the patent rights throughout Great Britain, the Colonies, America and France. As these were situated away from the hotel, a covered way was constructed to enable them to be used at any time.

Like all its predecessors, Thames Riviera had to start off with a grander than grand opening celebration, and on Friday 22 June 1928, as the *Surrey Comet* reported, 'a changed and brightened Tagg's Island opened with an inaugural dinner on Friday to a large and merry gathering that celebrated the event with such goodwill as to inspire hopes of its popularity and success. The efforts that have been made to ensure the appeal of this new riverside playground have been marked by the exercise of taste and enterprise on the part of Mr Herbert Cyril, the proprietor, and certainly every comfort was provided for the guests so hospitably received on Friday'.

The dinner was served to the accompaniment of music by Jack Hylton's Riviera Band, there was dancing in the world-famous ballroom, a display of acrobatic skating and ice dancing on the new rink, and d'Amato's Venetian Orchestra played from a gondola on the river. The floodlit tennis court proved so popular that play was still going on at midnight.

Herbert Cyril tried hard to find a ballet of ice-skaters in this country to perform in his new rink, but at that time there were no English professionals performing this type of entertainment. As a result he was forced to employ a troupe of German skaters. The rink was a terrific success but, after the second week, he was informed by the Government that he must send the company back to Germany, and accordingly he was compelled to close the skating at a dead loss of £10,000. Undoubtedly he was the first British impresario to realise the potentialities of ice-entertainment, and the elaborate pantomimes on ice which were now put on are in some way the culmination of his foresight.

Perhaps it was thought that changing the name of the island would reflect in a change of fortune. But the only effect it seemed to have was to bring the pains on earlier. Thames Riviera's first reign was, in fact, to be the shortest on record. Within six weeks of opening it had gone the way of its predecessors. The mortgagee put in a receiver and the luckless Mr Cyril found himself appearing in Bankruptcy Buildings, with debts of over £76,000, and assets of only £16,000.

The mortgagee was a firm called the United Kingdom Advertising Company, who had advanced some £11,000. Seeing their money fast disappearing, and the possibility of the lease being forfeited, which was the only security they possessed, they persuaded the receiver to allow them to take over the lease and run it themselves.

In 1930 Thames Riviera was opened up again, and it was the same old story told once again. A lot of money was spent in smartening up the island. 'The sumptuously appointed hotel', it was reported, 'the charmingly appointed ballroom and theatre, with what is regarded as one of the finest floors in Europe, cosy alcoves for suppers and a restful balcony; the covered tennis courts, badminton courts, putting greens, sea sand beach, pretty lawns and gardens, and facilities for bathing and boating, have all been overhauled and brought into perfect condition, and access to the island for cars is made simple by a huge electrically-driven ferry'.

The project was again launched with a splendid first night. This time there was a blend of banquet, ball, cabaret and cinema, allegedly the first time that such a concoction had ever been put on in Britain. Even the films shown were somewhat of a mixture: Mickey Mouse, a newsreel of the Football Cup Final, and several other small films, and to startle the assembled guests, Mr A.E. Bundy, the chairman and prime mover of the company, appeared on the screen himself, talking about the new venture. He emphasised that the comfort of patrons would receive the closest personal attention, and went on 'I am sensible of the difficulties I am confronted with, but I am not without hope that I shall be successful'. Even when chided with the island's past history he was full of optimism. 'When Bundy pulls the strings', he rejoined, 'they are the strings of success'. How far that optimistic boast was to go we shall see.

In 1933 the island hit the headlines again. One of the Sunday newspapers had run a series of articles concerning the river, and how it had become a place for hilarious groups of young people from London. Referring to 'gay mixed parties of men and girls to the more secluded reaches of the Thames', and saying that the 'regular devotees of the all night parties are those who, still unsatiated in their lust for excitement when London's West End restaurants and clubs close their doors soon after midnight, turn to the Thames to carry on their amusement'. Although they specifically spoke of the Thames from Sunbury to Henley, unfortunately they referred to it as the 'Thames Riviera'. Mr Bundy quickly seized on these words and brought an action against the paper, alleging that the words libelled them, and inferred that Tagg's Island was a place frequented by immoral persons where scandalous bathing and dancing took place. It was an opinion with which the judge apparently concurred, for he awarded the company damages of £1,000.

Still, even this bonus was not enough to keep the Thames Riviera solvent, and in 1935 the island was taken over by a further company, the managing director of which was Mr Charles Clore. This was one of the first enterprises of a man whose name was to become synonymous with property speculation. The company was registered with a nominal capital of £3,000, but only two £1 shares were issued. A considerable sum of money had to be spent on redecorating the hotel but, as the company had no money itself, it had to rely on loans. The hotel was re-opened on 4 June, under the new title 'Casino Hotel'; again the change of name did nothing to help its success; again within six months the company was compulsorily wound up. According to *The Times* 'Mr Clore attributed the insolvency of the company to the failure of the public to accord its patronage to the hotel, but in the opinion of the Official Receiver, it was due in no small measure to the fact that it was allowed to embark on a speculative business without the provision of any working capital'.

The lease was then acquired by a firm called Taggs Island Properties Ltd, who continued to run the hotel, still called 'Casino', until the Second World War came along. In 1941 it was acquired by Mr William Hurlock, of AC Cars Ltd of Thames Ditton who, in the following year, also purchased the freehold from Mr C.W. Kent, thereby terminating a connection which the Kent family had had with the island for almost a century. The buildings now took on a wartime aspect. The magnificent skating rink and the covered tennis courts were adapted as a factory, with a manufacturing floor area of about 26,000 square feet. For the rest of the war it did yeoman service in the production of munitions. A road bridge was supplied and constructed by the Ministry of Supply, connecting the island with the Middlesex bank, to ease access for delivery of material.

When peace came, the Casino Hotel was reconditioned and opened up to visitors, although the other buildings still carried out for a number of years useful national work in the manufacture of AC's renowned three-wheeled invalid carriages for the Ministry of Pensions. They also manufactured other types of cars. For instance, on the island were produced the four de-luxe trains which carried passengers along the mile-long pier at Southend.

The next few years were probably the most tranquil in the island's history. In 1956, however, it was sold, and since that time its story has been one of continuing strife. The ownership has changed hands several times, each time with a stiff escalation of the selling price; in 1956 it was £75,000; by 1967, £90,000; and in 1970 £120,000. There have been lawsuits, bankruptcies, proposals, and planning applications *ad nauseum*. In 1965 a scheme to open a gambling casino was stopped by a court action at the eleventh hour, after another £2,200 had been spent, and 300 guests had been invited to 'a bit of a flourish'. A few years later a Mr Ramsawak Doon Pandit proposed to build 'the finest hotel in Southern England', but it came to nought.

In 1965 the bridge was declared unsafe and, just three days before Christmas, the supports gave way and it settled down into the river, to the aggravation of the houseboat dwellers and AC Cars, who were still using the island, all of whom had to use the ferry again. There were all sorts of rumours about the bridge, accusations and counter accusations, and denial of responsibility. It was finally reconstructed by the owners.

In 1970 an application for planning permission for a one million pound development was submitted to pull down the old hotel, which, with only just over thirty bedrooms, was considered uneconomic, and to build a new one five storeys high, with 244 bedrooms, two swimming pools, sauna bath, floating restaurants, sports centre and parking for 250 cars. In spite of opposition from the Surrey side of the river and from the houseboat dwellers threatened with eviction, this plan was approved by Richmond Council in February 1971.

Within a month of having the plans passed the hotel was demolished. Before the bulldozers moved in, however, there was an orgy of nostalgia from a band of old music hall stars, who held a party of farewell. The hotel was already rotting from having been left idle, and through the battered dome water dripped onto the gilded mouldings, painted ceilings, and famous dancing floor. Nevertheless, old stagers spent a sentimental day reminiscing on Karsino in its palmy days – performers like Jack Melville, who joined Karno's company in 1904 and had trodden these boards almost sixty years before, and who that very day was celebrating his 88th birthday. The celebrated stage was ripped up and ceremoniously cut into portions to be given to the famous pupils from Karno's school and, as few of them could come to the celebrations themselves, their pieces were accepted on their behalf by other stars. The gift for Charlie Chaplin was given to Jimmy Jewell, who said he would send it on to the great comedian. Billy Russell, another of Karno's company, accepted a piece for Sandy Powell. Roy Hudd received Fred Emney's souvenir, and Ethel Revnell, who herself lived on a houseboat moored to the island, and was well-known in Molesey, especially for the work she performed for the Welcome Club, took a piece for Jimmy Nervo. Jack Melville proposed a toast to Karno, 'the man who put more laughs into Britain than anybody else', and the BBC made a film of the whole occasion.

So what *The Times* described as 'one of the strangest buildings in Britain', came tumbling down, and an era of British catering and entertainment history was but a pile of rubble.

However, in spite of planning permission, and in spite of having razed the old hotel to the ground, the proposed new hotel and sports centre was never proceeded with, and in 1974 fresh plans were submitted for a different type of development. This envisaged the building of blocks of flats up to four storeys high, surrounded by maisonettes and houses, some of them overhanging the river on the Molesey side, a total of 138 homes. A scheme of such intensive development was bound to cause considerable controversy and bitter opposition. In 1976 the developer went bankrupt, but new proposals were made.

With its future in doubt, in the 1970s the island's forthcoming history looked likely to be just as disputatious as its past. Then it remained desolate and overgrown, a bleak descendant of the glory it once was, with absolutely nothing to show for the millions of pounds which had been poured into it. As one stood and surveyed the ravaged scene, it was just possible that we might catch a glimpse of a group of shadowy figures, and among them recognise the features of Harvey and Kent, of Barrie, Tagg, Karno, Alexander, Cyril, Bundy, Charlie Clore and Leon Bronesky, all standing around and dropping fivers into a bottomless pit. For this surely was the most expensive piece of devastation in the whole world. It was constructed out of the debris of men's hopes and fortunes. And if we are prone to believe in legends we could even have seen circling above, the spirit of an evicted squatter, still cursing the men, the island, and all who were responsible for its being dispossessed of home and hearth many years ago. However, by 1988, Tagg's Island had become a paradise for houseboats and wildlife – almost a return to its idyllic past of long ago.

The Hotel and Ballroom at Tagg's Island, when it had become the Casino.

# THE "KARSINO,"
## HAMPTON COURT.
### Sole Proprietor: FRED KARNO.

## THE MOST DELIGHTFUL SPOT IN ENGLAND,

Situate upon an Island (Tagg's Island) in the beautiful stretch of the Thames between Molesey and Sunbury Lock, with Hurst Park on the Surrey Bank and on the Middlesex shore the natural beauties of Bushey Park. To reach the Island a fine flotilla of

### FERRY BOATS,

Both for MOTOR CARS and PASSENGER TRAFFIC, controlled by experienced workmen, ply to and fro daily **FREE OF CHARGE**, Sundays and Holidays excepted, when the finest Regimental Bands in the Kingdom dispense music of the highest order at 3 and 7 p.m., for which the Return Ferry Charge is 6d.

Amongst others engaged for the season the following may be mentioned:—

| H.M. Band of the 1st Life Guards | H.M. Band of the Grenadiers | H.M. Band of the 2nd Life Guards | H.M. Band of the Royal Fusiliers |
|---|---|---|---|
| "   "   " Irish   " | "   "   " Scots Guards | "   "   " Coldstream   " | "   "   " Black Watch |
| "   "   " Royal Marines | "   "   " Royal Engineers | "   "   " 19th Hussars | "   "   " 15th Hussars |

Jimmy Glover's Orchestra, &c.

### THE GROUNDS AND TERRACES,
Are arranged in Floral Profusion, and at night when

## ILLUMINATED WITH MYRIADS OF COLOURED ELECTRIC LIGHTS IN THE FOLIAGE,

this ideal River Resort appears a veritable Fairyland.

The "KARSINO" has been constructed to give the greatest possible pleasure to its patrons, irrespective of the elements, so that—**WET OR FINE**—Comfort, Hospitality and Enjoyment will always be found in

### THE PALM COURT,

with its beautifully decorated Ceiling illustrative of the finest Thames Scenery.

### CAFE CONCERTS and ENTERTAINMENTS

are given daily at 3 & 8 by the most High-Class Vocalists, Vaudeville Artistes and Musicians, admission to which upon week days is 6d., 1s., & 2s.

### THE KARSINO ORCHESTRA,

under the direction of Mr. J. H. SQUIRE, plays at each of these Entertainments, also at the **FREE CAFE CONCERTS ON SUNDAYS**.

LUNCHEONS, DINNERS, TEAS and REFRESHMENTS are served from the

### NEW ISLAND HOTEL

(upon the balconies), in the Palm Court and Grounds, at moderate prices, when a perfect cuisine with high-class service may be relied upon.

The "Karsino" is also equipped with an extensive and up-to-date

### BOATHOUSE,

from which new magnificently-appointed BOATS, PUNTS, DINGHEYS, CANOES AND LAUNCHES may be hired by the hour, day, week or season, at most moderate charges. Boats built, housed, cleaned and varnished at the shortest notice. Boat Fittings of every description supplied.

*VISITORS residing in the district have most easy access to "The Karsino" by TRAMS or BUSES that pass the Ferry Landing Stage every few minutes. A Table of the best trains can be obtained upon application from any of the attendants at The "Karsino."*

VISITORS to the "Karsino" arriving by boats, have same moored and cared for, during their sojourn, free of charge at all times. This also applies to Motor Cars which are housed in the

### "KARSINO GARAGE,"

where petrol and accessories are always obtainable.

All communications concerning The New Island Hotel should be addressed to the Manager of same, Mr. JAMES NIGG, whilst those referring to THE PALM COURT, GROUNDS & BOATING, should be addressed to Mr. JOHN H. L. SHERRATT, the Manager of these departments.

Telephone: 1 Molesey.                                                                 Telegrams: "Karsino," Hampton Court.

OPPOSITE: Karno advertises Karsino.

ABOVE: A quite corner in the Karsino.

CENTRE: the Karsino.

BELOW: A continental atmosphere pervaded the grounds in 1930.

ABOVE: Jack Hylton's Riviera Band at the Karsino, 22 June 1928 – the Karsino was to be the Thames Riviera. BELOW: The Royal Flying Corps at Hurst Park in 1915.

# *Willow'd Aytes*

As we continue along the towpath, we notice on our left hand side, immediately after Molesey Boat Club, a piece of open space, which is partly laid out as a children's playground. This land was given to the district by Mr W.E.A. Hurlock, of AC Cars, in September 1953, to preserve the amenity of the riverside area.

The road which separates this land from the cricket ground was originally laid down across open fields in 1874 by Tom Tagg, to provide access to the then newly opened Island Hotel. Today it remains privately owned, although the Borough, as owners of Mr Hurlock's gift, have a corporate private right of way over it. It is now called 'Graburn Way', a tribute to Lt Col 'Willy' Graburn, a man with cricket in his blood. He became instructor to the Surrey County Club at the Oval in 1892, and was captain of East Molesey Cricket Club from 1908 to 1920, when he took over as secretary. 'His batting', it was said, 'was always graceful and elegant and stylish'.

East Molesey Cricket Club must surely have one of the most delightfully situated pitches in the country, which adds greatly to the pleasure and enjoyment of lounging around on a hot summer's day watching others run about. The club's modern pavilion is only marred by one thing – the date 1730 painted across its facade. Whilst it is true that cricket was played in Molesey in the early part of the eighteenth century, that took place on Molesey Hurst, some half a mile or so away in West Molesey. The present cricket ground was never part of the Hurst, and it is sad to see a club with an honourable history going back over a hundred years, making such a claim.

In 1871 a cricket team calling itself East Molesey played on Hampton Court Green and later on 'a meadow opposite Tagg's Island'. However, this was not today's ground, but a piece of land nearer to the lock, which was rented from Tom Tagg. The club lasted only a short while and, as they owed the rent, Mr Tagg distrained on the club's gear in lieu of the money. The late Col Tagg remembers as a boy 'annexing' the bats, stumps, and other paraphernalia, with which he and his friends played on the island.

In March 1879 it was announced 'A cricket club is in course of formation under the presidency of the Rev. W.F. Reynolds, vicar. From the present appearance it will be an undoubted success'. At first the club played on a piece of ground loaned by Mr Herbert Andrews in Molesey Park, behind today's Woolworth's store. A few years later it moved to the present pitch, which was hired from Mr Kent, and shared with a lacrosse team. The club now owns the freehold and the land should be preserved for willow and leather for all times.

One of the pleasantest features of the cricket field used to be a ponderous row of trees skirting the ground and dividing it from the towpath. Sadly these mighty creations have now all gone – humbled by the little Dutch elm beetle.

In 1917 these trees were the scene of a most extraordinary mishap. On Whit Sunday a pilot from the Royal Flying Corps training camp, which had been set up on Hurst Park during the Kaiser's War, went up and was performing acrobatics for the delectation of holiday crowds along the riverside, when his undercarriage caught on the telephone wires crossing to Tagg's Island, and the machine, a biplane, crashed head-on into the trees. The crowds on the towpath expected to see the plane come hurtling to the ground, with its occupant either killed or badly injured. Yet by some miracle the impact was so forceful that the machine remained firmly fixed in the branches. The *Surrey Comet* takes up the story: 'Ropes were obtained, P.C. Walter Baker, of the Molesey Section-house, climbing the tree, and after the officer, who was strapped to his seat, had fastened one around him, he was safely lowered to the ground. Beyond suffering from shock, he appeared to be little worse for the accident. The propeller of the biplane was completely smashed, as were other parts of the machine. When the aviator reached the ground he was taken to the Karsino, where he received numerous congratulations upon his lucky escape. Under the tree into which the machine crashed was a rustic seat, upon which a lady was sitting, but on hearing the crash she quickly made her escape'. (P.C. Walter Baker was the author's father.)

To the west of the cricket field the land opens out, and we now have the choice of continuing along the gravelled towpath close to the river or treading the soft, green, meadow turf. This long, narrow field between the towpath and the old racecourse was another of Mr Hurlock's gifts to the district. It was presented in December 1946, 'to preserve the picturesque nature of this part of the River Thames and to prevent bungalows and similar structures being built on it'. On a manorial map of Molesey dated 1781 this meadow is called 'More Hampton Shott'. The other meadows between here and Hurst Road, which were later incorporated into the racecourse, also had interesting names, such as: 'Beggars Bush', 'Broomhill', 'Broom Shott' and 'Pink Hill'.

The channel between the Molesey bank and Tagg's Island along this reach was at one time known as 'The Gull', a name which is often heard of along the Thames, for a narrow fast-moving stream of water.

The little ait just above Tagg's Island was known as 'Duck Eyot' or 'Swan's Nest Island', recalling the lines of Molesey's own poet – Joseph Palmer:

'The Thames, majestic! flowing by her side,
Where num'rous swans in stately freedom glide;
The willow'd Aytes their annual nests contain,
Where undisturb'd the mother birds remain'.

Old maps show the island much larger than it is now, although the fact that the boundary between Hampton and East Molesey passes between the two islands, making Tagg's in Middlesex and Swan's Nest in Surrey, seems to suggest that at one time this was the main stream of the river. The flow of current picking up silt here and depositing it there, meant that the contour of the river was continually changing, as indeed it has done even in the lifetime of the present writer. To prevent this erosion and to keep the channel clear for navigation the Thames Conservancy has now protected both this island and the head of Tagg's with a barrier of camp shuttering. Here in the summer one can usually see one or two boats moored and their occupants enjoying a picnic on the grass.

Above Swan's Nest Island the river starts on a wide left-hand sweep, which continues for half a mile or so, and broadens out into a grand vista, with the tower of Hampton Church peeking over the trees, and the noble villas and verdant lawns of the opposite bank completing altogether a picture unsurpassed for beauty anywhere else on the Thames.

The water's edge here is rutted by little coves, covered with beds of reeds and lilies, the widened river becomes more sluggish and:

'Flowing so softly that scarcely it seems to be flowing,
But the reeds of the low little island are bent to its going'.         Isa Craig Knox

This part of the river is a paradise for anglers. A book called *The Lower and Mid Thames; where and how to fish it,* published in 1894, says 'Swan's Nest Island, is above Taggs Island, and the water in this vicinity holds jack, one of over 20lb. being taken there some years ago. These specimen fish are, however, a rarity in any part of the Thames. A favourite roach swim is opposite Garrick's Villa, and bream may sometimes be taken there. The angler will see that from a pipe fixed in the wall some spring water falls into the Thames. He should fix his boat or punt just opposite. Hampton Deeps, which hold jack, roach and bream, extend from Molesey Weir to Garrick Villa, a distance of 1500 yards; and there is an eddy under the willow tree at the end of Garrick's lawn from which a jack or two may sometimes be taken'.

On the Hampton side of the river, shaded by the branches of a massive cedar tree, and with a velvet lawn stretching right down to the water's edge, is a large house known as Garrick's House, not to be confused with Garrick's Villa, which is the next house upstream and on the other side of Hampton Court Road. This house used to be called The Cedars. It received its present name because it was once owned by David Garrick junior, the nephew of his more famous namesake.

Downstream from Garrick's House, where now a green bank slopes sharply down from the road to the river, there stood until a few years ago another rambling old mansion, which was known as St Albans. This is alleged to have been built by Charles II for Nell Gwyn, and named after their son, the first Duke of St Albans. 'Nelly', so the story goes 'stood at a window with her baby son in her arms and, looking down at her kindly lover below threatened to throw the child out unless he was instantly given a title, whereupon Charles II called out loudly, "save the Duke of St. Albans" '. The house certainly contained some eighteenth century work, but was chiefly of much later date, and – as a well-researched booklet by Mr A.F. Kelsall, published by the Twickenham Local History Society, points out – it was never occupied either by Nell Gwyn or her son. It was, in fact, a later Duke of St Albans after whom it was named.

The story seems to have been invented and nurtured by the novelist Winifred Graham, a prolific writer in the early part of this century, who lived in the house for many years. There are no less than ninety-three books credited to her in the British Library index, and her life here is told in the trilogy of her autobiography, the most interesting features of which are the photographs of the house, both inside and out. She seems to have written so many novels that her whole life appears to devolve into a fantasy, and it is sometimes difficult to distinguish fact from fiction.

The house was substantially altered in the 1920s by Theodore Cory, Miss Graham's husband, a wealthy businessman with extensive interests in coal and shipping, who completely transformed the inside, removing walls, replacing them with Corinthian pillars (said to have come from Hurst House, West Molesey, together with some Adam fireplaces), and lining other walls with genuine old oak panelling brought from elsewhere, thereby giving the interior a luxury little to be expected from the nondescript pot-pourri of styles exhibited outside.

When Mr Cory died in 1961, he left the house to the Borough of Twickenham to be preserved as a memorial to his wife, but unfortunately with no endowment to sustain it. Equally unfortunately neither Twickenham nor its successor, the London Borough of Richmond upon Thames, possessed either the capital or the inclination to preserve the house, and in 1972, then in a state of imminent collapse, it was demolished and the site incorporated into the riverside gardens. Nevertheless an elegant brick shelter has been erected as a memorial.

Above Garrick's House, moored close to the Middlesex bank, rides the last remnant of the Golden Age of the houseboats, *Astoria* – Fred Karno's home – probably the most luxurious floating house ever known on the Thames. This was the houseboat which Karno had had built in 1913. After Karno's collapse she was sold, and in 1932 came into the hands of yet another great music hall artist, Vesta Victoria, the comedienne who made famous such songs as *Daddy wouldn't buy me a Bow-wow, Waiting at the Church* and *Poor John.*

Vesta resided on *Astoria*, and died in April 1951. The houseboat was sold, reputedly for a sum of £14,000. However, the new owner was not connected with the music hall, he was a business man, and disliked the publicity that life on a famous houseboat on a famous island brought. Seeking private waters, he had his home towed up to this more sequestered place, where he was less likely to be peeped and peered at by a prying public.

Here *Astoria* now sits, her magnificent panelling, marble fittings and plush furnishings intact, although she has a new hull, with some of the elaborate framework gone. As we stand on the Molesey bank we can now take full advantage of her ninety-two feet of glory, and with little effort still picture the famous parties on a summer evening, the awning spread, the upper deck awash with a mass of humanity all swaying and gyrating to the lilt of Jack Hylton's music.

ABOVE: East Molesey Cricket ground. BELOW: The new Pavilion.
OPPOSITE: The souvenir score card of 19 June 1949 – East Molesey v New Zealand.

98

FIRST BIG MATCH OF THE EAST MOLESEY CRICKET CLUB SEASON, 1949

President: B. M. TURNER, Esq.　　　　Captain: JAMES THOMPSON.

## SOUVENIR SCORE CARD - 6d.

### East Molesey Memorial Cricket Ground

EAST MOLESEY, SURREY　　Phone: Molesey 2542

# EAST MOLESEY v. NEW ZEALAND

JUNE 19th, 1949

Hours of Play: 11.30 a.m.—6 p.m.

**PROCEEDS IN AID OF GRABURN MEMORIAL PAVILION FUND**

H.R.H. THE DUKE OF EDINBURGH honours the East Molesey Cricket Club with his presence, together with the LORD CHANCELLOR OF ENGLAND, the Rt. Hon. LORD JOWITT; the MINISTER OF DEFENCE, the Rt. Hon. A. V. ALEXANDER, M.P.; the HOME SECRETARY, the Rt. Hon. J. CHUTER EDE, M.P. and the Honourable the AGENTS GENERAL for QUEENSLAND, VICTORIA, SOUTH AUSTRALIA and WESTERN AUSTRALIA, with H.E. The DEPUTY HIGH COMMISSIONER FOR AUSTRALIA.

Presentation of Players to H.R.H. THE DUKE OF EDINBURGH at 2.20 p.m.

*Cricket has been played on the East Molesey Ground since 1693.*

### EAST MOLESEY

| # | BATSMEN | HOW OUT | BOWLER | SCORE |
|---|---|---|---|---|
| 1 | †R. W. V. ROBINS (Molesey, Middx. & England). | | | |
| 2 | ERIC EDWARDS (Molesey) | C. Cave | Smith | 65 |
| 3 | A. SWIFT (Molesey) | | | |
| 4 | L. FISHLOCK (Surrey & England) | LBW | Donnelly | 22 |
| 5 | R. J. ATTAWELL (Molesey) | B | " | 31 |
| 6 | B. CONSTABLE (Molesey & Surrey) | C. Donnelly | " | 50 |
| 7 | G. TRIBE (Colne & Australia) | Not Out | | 8 |
| 8 | W. ALLEY (Rawtenstall & New South Wales) | C. Mooney | Wallace | 58 |
| 9 | J. THOMPSON (Molesey) | | | |
| 10 | J. GODDARD (Molesey) | | | |
| 11 | K. CRACKNELL (Molesey) | | | |
| 12 | *J. M. A. PARKER (Molesey) | | | |

Reserves:
G. HOLLEY (Molesey)
R. TINDALL (Molesey)

Extras ... 7

Total 241 - 5 Dec.

Numbers do not necessarily indicate order of batting

Fall of Wickets............

Bowling Analysis ...　　O.　M.　R.　W.

### NEW ZEALAND

| # | BATSMEN | HOW OUT | BOWLER | SCORE |
|---|---|---|---|---|
| 1 | V. SCOTT (Auckland) | | | |
| 2 | B. SUTCLIFFE (Auckland) | | | |
| 3 | †W. HADLEE (Canterbury) | | | |
| 4 | W. WALLACE (Auckland) | Bowled | Tribe | 45 |
| 5 | M. P. DONNELLY (Warwickshire & Taranaki) | Bowled | " | 8 |
| 6 | F. SMITH (Canterbury) | C. Cracknell | " | 12 |
| 7 | G. RABONE (Wellington) | | | |
| 8 | T. T. BURTT (Canterbury) | LBW | " | 44 |
| 9 | *F. MOONEY (Wellington) | C. Thompson | " | 14 |
| 10 | H. CAVE (Wellington) | C. | | 3 |
| 11 | J. COWIE (Auckland) | | | |
| 12 | J. REID (Wellington) | B | Cracknell | 70 |
| 13 | F. CRESSWELL (Wellington) | | | |
| 14 | J. A. HAYES (Auckland) | | | 7 |
| 15 | C. C. BURKE (Auckland) | LBW | Tribe | 0 |

Extras ...

Total 242

Numbers do not necessarily indicate order of batting

Fall of Wickets............

Bowling Analysis ...　　O.　M.　R.　W.

† Captain　　　　* Wicketkeeper

Umpires: H. WOOLLEY and A. G. BROADBENT.　　Scorer: R. R. SKELHORN.

*The 2nd Big Match of the Season is v. Peter Smith's Essex xi July 3rd*

99

ABOVE: Garrick's House. BELOW: St Albans in 1950 – it was demolished in 1972, the site incorporated into what are now the riverside gardens. OPPOSITE ABOVE: Mr and Mrs Cory at St Albans in 1950 and CENTRE: their dining room, with its oak panelling. BELOW: The *Astoria,* moored at Garricks Lawn today.

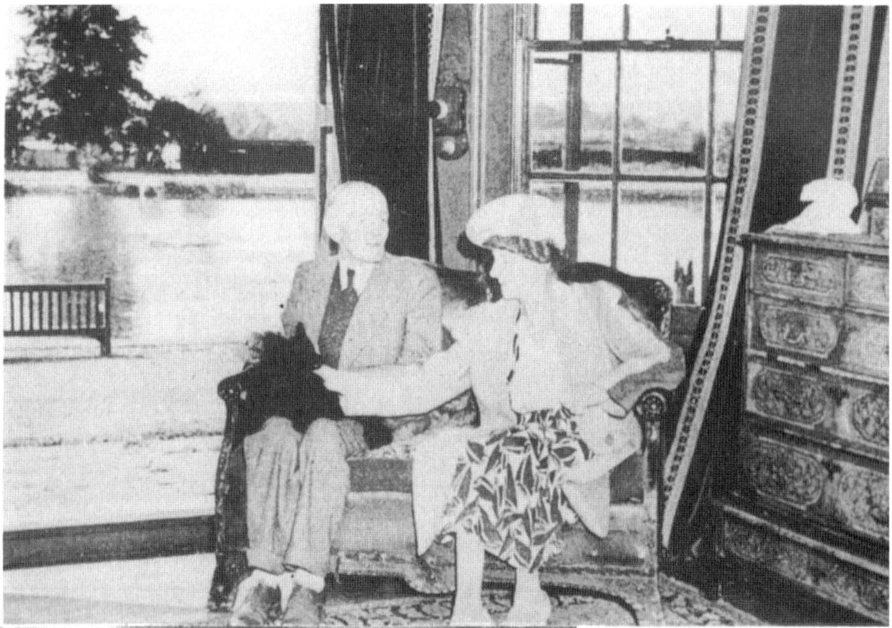

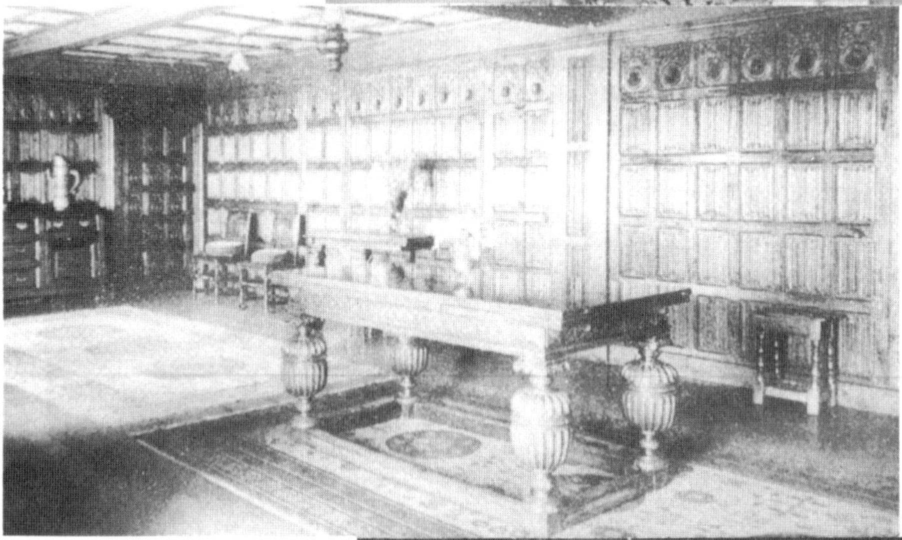

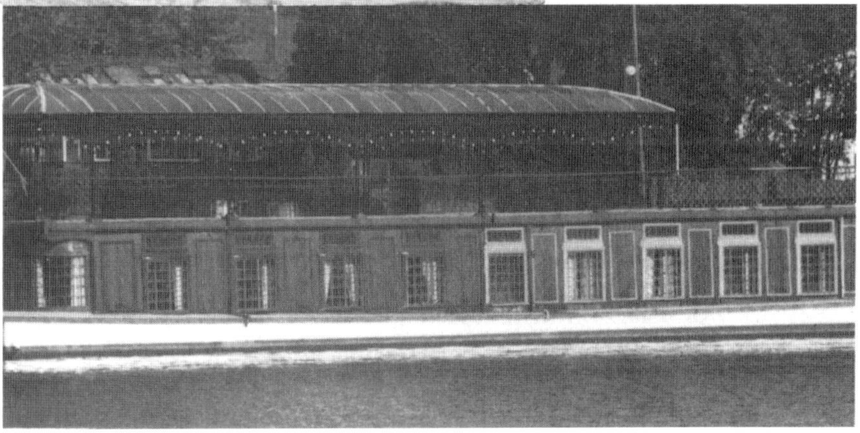

ABOVE: 'A View of the Seat of the late David Garrick Esq... with the Temple of Shakespeare in the Garden' and BELOW: Medland's engraving of 1783.

# Garrick's Villa

'Hampton we pass, where Davy Garrick came
With histrionic triumphs all aflame;
His loved and honoured spirit long hath flown,
But still this spot his memory doth own'.

E. Derry, *Four Days on the Thames* (1899)

There is no doubt that the best view of Hampton is obtained from this side of the river, and (as every topographer of the Thames emphasises) the most dominant feature of the landscape is Garrick's Villa. When viewed across the water, the old mansion seems to preside over the whole scene, like a massive squatting hen, viewing with pride her scattered brood. Originally known as Hampton House, it was acquired by Garrick, perhaps the most famous actor ever to tread the boards of any stage, in 1754. Here he resided, entertained the famous, and acted the life of a country gentleman, until his death in 1779. His widow continued to occupy the house until 1822, when she too died.

Garrick's first concern was to turn the house, which was then a much meaner affair, into a residence grand enough for the most eminent actor in Britain. He asked Robert Adam, to whom he was already well-known, to make some additions and improvements. The result was that the house was given a classical facade, with a Corinthian arcade surmounted by a portico and pediment, and on either side pilasters and a cornice. It was supposed to have been based on the palace of the emperor Diocletian at Split in Dalmatia, which Adam had surveyed in 1757. Capability Brown was employed to lay out the gardens and build the orangery. The Adam brothers and Chippendale designed the interior and furniture.

It was probably Capability also who planned what undoubtedly is the pleasantest feature of the scene – the little octagonal Grecian temple, with its Ionic porch, which nestles on the lawn not far from the water's edge. It was intended as a summer house and home for the statue of Shakespeare which Roubiliac had executed for Garrick at a cost of 300 guineas.

The lawn on which the temple stands was all part of the Villa's grounds, but it presented Garrick with somewhat of a dilemma. The ground between the temple and the house was transversed by the Staines to Kingston road. Garrick wanted to cross over privately between the two. He had seen the ornamental bridge which had been built over the Portsmouth Road at Painshill, Cobham, and rather fancied a similar structure. But the two situations were entirely different; Painshill is built on a hillside, with the road low down, and Hampton is on the flat. The engineering problems really ruled out a bridge, and it was Dr Johnson, who was visiting Garrick at the time, who finally settled the matter, with a famous retort: 'Davy! Davy! what can't be overdone, may be underdone', and a tunnel was decided on.

But what a tunnel it turned out to be, all ornamental with fantastic stonework and coral in the form of a grotto. The arched entrance into the 'fairy-footed passage' as it was called in 1797, can be seen from our towpath, just to the left of *Astoria*. The lawn is not part of a public garden, but the tunnel is stopped up by a grille to prevent access.

Johnson's other well-known remark about the house which has survived, is supposed to have been uttered when the great lexicographer was first shown over the house and its beauties: 'Ah, David, it is the leaving of such a place that makes a death-bed terrible'. When Garrick did leave the house and this earth, he was worth £100,000, and he was buried near to Shakespeare's monument in Westminster Abbey. Roubiliac's Shakespearean statue he bequeathed to the British Museum, where it may still be seen. But so that the temple could still fulfil the function for which it was created, its place was taken by a stone replica.

In 1774, so the *Gentleman's Magazine* tells us, Garrick gave a splendid night entertainment, or 'Fête Champêtre', to which all the celebrities of the day were invited. There were fireworks and a concert of music. The Temple of Shakespeare' and gardens were illuminated with 6,000 lamps. What a magnificent sight and sound it must have presented from where we now stand on the Molesey bank.

At the beginning of this century, when the tramway was being laid between Hammersmith and Hampton Court, the highway needed to be widened to take the tracks, but the owner of Garrick's Villa refused to sell just a strip wide enough to expand the road, and insisted that the company purchase the whole property. Thereupon the chairman of the tramways, Sir Clifton Robinson, annexed the property as his own residence. Sir Clifton had a personal tram for his sole use, so that he could travel around the system, and had points fitted on the lines outside the house, so that his tram could be driven directly into a private 'garage' by the side of his residence. This entrance could still be seen up to a few years ago.

Every year Sir Clifton and Lady Robinson gave a garden party for the wives and children of London United Tramway workers in the grounds of the Villa. From all over the north-west of the metropolis special trams arrived laden with dependants, about 3,000 of them, all eager for the treat. One car carried the band from Hanwell depôt, playing all the way from the top deck. When they arrived at Hampton they found that an enormous marquee had been erected on the lawn by the side of the house, with rows of tables laid out with comestibles of all descriptions. Later a 'farcical regatta', with all sorts of water sports, was arranged for the entertainment of the crowd and, to crown the day, before the weary families returned home, each child was presented by Lady Clifton herself with his or her own box of chocolates. The house has now been turned into a series of Flats, but in such a way as to preserve its eighteenth century character.

Snuggling beneath the shadow of Garrick's Villa and the temple, lies the island which Garrick bought, and which is now named after him. Earlier it was known as Shank's Ait or Higher Ait. It was at one time much lower and covered by willows and osiers, which were haunted by families of otters.

The islets along this reach were used extensively for the cultivation of osiers for the manufacture of basketry and cane furniture. The beds were cut in the summer time, and the withies, some of them as much as twelve feet long, were peeled on special instruments and left to bleach in the sun. Stacks of golden yellow rods, neatly assorted into lengths, could be seen glistening in the sunlight, or when the air was too dry and sultry, laying in the stream of the river to preserve their natural pliance, and to prevent their becoming hard and brittle.

Soon after the end of the Kaiser's war, to its eternal disgrace, the island was let out in small plots for the erection of weekend bungalows, some of which are merely squalid shacks, and give a sense of lasting shame to an otherwise delightful view.

On a fine winter's day in 1796 Joseph Palmer, the man after whom a school in West Molesey used to be named, stood like us on the towpath and surveyed the scene, as we do now; 'Then, turning to the right', he wrote, 'I with reverence met the Temple to Shakespeare – I had then, partly through yew-trees, and over walls separating the high road, bound with rich coats of ivy, a good sight of the retired villa – and well it looks – In this stage I had the satisfaction to recollect the following lines, by Mr Sheridan:

"The Yew-tree and Cypress, for sorrow renowned,
And tear-dropping Willow, shall near thee be found;
All Nature shall droop, and united complain,
That Shakespear in Garrick hath died over again".

'Then throwing the eye along small but beautiful lawns, and over the stately trees in Bushey Park, whose branches swell with the rising road, and lessen again, until it reposes on Hampton's magnificent palace'.

'A retrograde move of the head gave East Molesey's modest steeple; backed at a distance by a long chain of hill, in which Epsom Downs are particularly distinguished. Immediately dropping the eye; Hampton's white bridge; with the palace, near one extremity, and a white house at the other, from whatever station seen, are happily situated to be admired'.

ABOVE: The octagonal Grecian temple at Garrick's Villa;
BELOW: the Villa in 1974.

LEFT: Garrick bequeathed this life-size statue of Shakespeare to the British Museum; he commissioned it from Roubiliac in 1758, for his Temple of Shakespeare. RIGHT: Garrick's grotto. BELOW: The original Shanks, or Higher Ait became Garrick's Island.

# *The Bathing Station*

On our own bank, from 1890 until some twenty years ago the tow-path was hemmed in by the ugly monotonous fence of Hurst Park racecourse, by the side of which stood the Molesey Bathing Station.

It was during the Victorian era that river bathing became popular, and men were allowed to swim in the Thames before eight in the morning and after eight at night. But there were continual complaints, and some prosecutions, after genteel ladies walking along the towpath espied men bathing at other times. In 1901 the council established a bathing station on Ash Island, and later another alongside the river Mole at West Molesey. The Ash Island station seems to have faded out about the time of the First World War and, when that conflict was concluded, several requests were made to re-establish a station on the Thames. On the suggestion of the Thames Conservancy a site was chosen just a little below Garrick's Island. A piece of ground was rented by the council from the Hurst Park Club at a nominal rent of £1 a year, and on 27 May 1925 the station was opened for public use.

The present author recalls many happy hours spent as a youth around this spot. Few things are pleasanter when one is young and the weather is warm than to plunge into a nice cool stream. The target of all the boys was a tiny islet which formerly stood at the tail of Garrick's Ait. The compulsion to get across that little channel was amazing, for to reach the island one had to go out of one's depth and that was the acid test of one's ability to swim. You had to have the confidence not only to get there, but to get back too. Not that there was much on the islet when you got there – just a little green patch, one solitary tree, and mud, mud which oozed through your toes. Nevertheless the first achievement was great, you were there, and that was the proof you were now a swimmer. For, as Oliver Wendell Holmes remarked: 'Leander swam the Hellespont – And I will swim this here'.

On a warm summer's evening the area around the bathing station was alive with activity. The river's edge bubbled with splashing youngsters in and out of the water, the raft rebounding to the feet of plunging divers, the more experienced swimmers out in the deep, the towpath milling with people who had already had their dip or who had only come to watch, and over all the geniality of the attendant – Mr McLachlan – 'Mac' to everybody. His benign superintendence saw to it that all troubles, cut toes, lost towels, cramp in the legs, swimmers in danger, everything great or small, was smoothly sorted out. But it was on a sunny Sunday when the bank was really at its best. All day long a mass of humanity stretched along the towpath for several hundred yards on either side of the bathing station. Camping, sun-bathing, picnicking, swimming or just lolling around, it was a colourful and noisy scene, the like of which one just does not see along the river now.

Over the years the little island, to which we used to swim, got smaller and smaller, the companionless tree died, and without these roots to hold it together rapidly eroded. It was finally dredged away soon after the end of the last war. The bathing station was destroyed by fire in 1966 and, because of changed attitudes towards river bathing, was never re-established.

ABOVE: William Beldham, Surrey and England cricketer, dominated the game for 35 years. BELOW: Cricket at Molesey Hurst in 1780 – this picture is held at the Marylebone CC.

# *The Hurst: Cradle of Cricket*

'And next the river flows past Moulsey Hurst;
And though no thicket cumbers now the ground,
Yet forest trees are scattered still, where erst
Nought but the gloomy glade and Druid's grove were found'.    John Stapleton (1878)

Molesey Hurst was originally a common meadow belonging to the Manor of Molesey Matham, of the type known as 'Lammas land'; that is, whilst hay was made there during the spring and summer, it was thrown open to all who had common rights to graze their cattle from Lammas Day (1 August) until Candlemas Day (2 February). From ancient maps it is to be seen that the Hurst lay entirely in the parish of West Molesey, stretching from the parish boundary at Hurst Lane to where Cherry Orchard Road is now, and on both sides of Hurst Road.

The earliest known mention of the Hurst is in 1249, when certain lands in West Molesey were transferred, including 'one meadow which lies by Herstegg'.

From the beginning of the eighteenth century the Hurst became the scene for many sporting encounters – cricket, archery, prize-fights, cock-fights, golf and horse-racing. Joseph Palmer, who lived in a house now demolished in New Road, and whose pen we have already quoted, wrote of 'that verdant level Moulsey Hurst; famous for all sports and lately for archery; the whistling arrows having the boldest range quiver in safety where they alight; and allowed too by cricketers from its elasticity, the best cricket ground in England'.

A game somewhat like cricket was played as early as the thirteenth century; mention is made of the boys of Guildford indulging in the sport in the time of the first Elizabeth. The game was born on the village greens and rustic commons.

At the end of the seventeenth century, however, a fundamental change took place. Cricket, once ignored by the aristocracy, was adopted by them as a leisure pursuit, and an outlet for their gambling habits. In the early days cricket matches were to be played for high stakes. Molesey Hurst offered excellent ground for these new supporters. It was within easy reach of the metropolis, central for the cricketing counties, and only a short distance from Hampton Court Palace, where lived Frederick Louis, Prince of Wales, a great patron of the sport, and the man who perhaps more than any other helped to grave the name Molesey deep on the cricketing map.

The earliest definite mention of cricket being played here that the author can trace is contained in an announcement which appeared in the *Saint James's Evening Post* on Tuesday 13 July 1731, that a match was arranged for the next day on 'Moulsey Hurst', between the men of Hampton and those of Brentford. It was further reported that 'above £500 is already laid on their heads, neither party having yet been beat'.

The September of that year saw several thousand people 'of both sexes' assembled on the Hurst to witness a side from the county of Surrey prove their superiority over the representatives of Kingston.

An exciting match took place in July 1733, in which Surrey just managed to beat Middlesex by three 'notches'. The Prince of Wales and 'several persons of distinction' were present, and 'his Royal Highness was pleased to order a guinea to be given to each man, for their great dexterity'. After this game was over a further match was arranged between the Prince and a Mr Stede, the Prince to choose an eleven from the men who had played that day, to match eleven that Mr Stede would pick from the county of Kent. A silver cup worth £30 was to be presented to the winners. This is the first recorded instance of a game played for such a cup. The match was played on the Hurst the following week, was won by the Prince's men, 'though not with so much ease as was expected, the odds being against Mr Stede's men at the beginning'.

During the next few years there are numerous mentions of matches being played here, often between teams picked by Royalty and gentry or representing various counties. At that time Molesey Hurst shared with Holt Pound at Farnham the distinction of being the chief grounds in Surrey.

In the eighteenth century cricket was not always played eleven-a-side, in fact there are several records of games on the Hurst with varying numbers of players from five-a-side to twenty-two. In June 1772, for instance, an eleven from Hampshire played twenty-two from other counties. This match started on a Monday and was played until Wednesday evening when, notwithstanding the great odds ranged against them, Hampshire were the winners.

In 1795 an eleven of Surrey played three three-day matches against thirteen of England. The first of these contests, played on 6, 7 and 8 July, was won by Surrey by 76 runs; the second and third, played consecutively 10 to 15 August, were both won by England, by 38 and 27 runs respectively. In the first innings of the latter match the Hon J. Tufton, one of the England side, is given out as 'l.b.w.', the first recorded appearance of that offence in the score books, although the rule was added during the revision of twenty-one years before, when it was found to be necessary because some batsmen were 'so shabby as to put their legs in the way and take advantage of the bowlers'.

On 3 August 1775 the Hurst was the scene of a extraordinary match – six married women against six spinsters which was won by the maidens, although it is recorded that one of the matrons knocked up seventeen runs. Many people were present to watch and the betting was said to be lively.

*Chambers' Journal* recounts an interesting story of cricket on the Hurst: 'Little did the City apothecary dream, when he offered to drive Lord Bute to the cricket match on Moulsey Hurst, that he was giving his country neighbour a lift in a double sense. Frederick, Prince of Wales, was a spectator at the match, and to amuse him while the players were waiting for the rain to give over, a rubber of whist was proposed. Noblemen being scarce, there was difficulty in making up the set, until someone remembered having seen Lord Bute on the ground. He was found and asked to join the royal party; and having played his cards so well, when the game was over the Prince invited him to Kew. There acquaintance soon ripened into friendship, and erelong the Scottish earl was all in all at Leicester House; adviser-in-chief to host and hostess, and director of the education of their son, the heir to the throne. With George III's accession came the rapid advancement; from Privy Councillor to Secretary of State, from Secretary of State to Premier; honours the best abused minister of his time might never have held but for taking a hand at whist on a rainy morning'.

Around 1755 a team calling themselves 'Moulsey' played several games, although it is doubtful if this was a properly organised club. The first attempt to form a regular club in Molesey seems to have been about 1787, when the famous Moulsey Hurst Cricket Club was inaugurated by a number of the most prominent cricketers of the day.

Among the club's members were some of the greatest exponents of the game including the Earl of Winchilsea, (who made some of the best scores for several seasons, and who at one time lived in Hurst House, a large mansion which formerly stood in New Road); Sir Peter Burrell, another good player; Lord Strathavon; the Hon Col Lennox, later duke of Richmond, who was a fine wicket-keeper, and who is noted as having fought a duel with the Duke of York; W. Bedster and Edward 'Lumpy' Stevens, who were both employed by Lord Tankerville at Mount Felix, Walton-on-Thames; and William 'Silver Billy' Beldham, perhaps the greatest batsman of the eighteenth century. 'Lumpy' Stevens received his nickname because he was 'a short man, round-shouldered and stout'. At one of the dinners of the Hambledon club, it was said, 'he did eat a whole apple pie'. John Nyron, the biographer of the Hambledon men, has this to say of him: 'he had no trick about him, but was as plain as a pikestaff in all his dealings', he died at the age of 84 and is buried in Walton churchyard. 'Silver Billy', so called because of his mop of straw-coloured hair, was a giant among cricketers, although not in size; Nyron says of him: 'William Beldham was a close set man, standing about five feet eight inches and a half. He had light-coloured hair, a fair complexion, and handsome as well as intelligent features. No one within my recollection could stop a ball better, or make more brilliant hits all over the ground. Wherever the ball was bowled there she was hit away, and in the most severe, venomous style. Besides this he was so remarkably safe a player; he was safer than the bank, for no mortal ever thought of doubting Beldham's stability. He would get in at the balls, and hit them away in a gallant style, but when he would cut them at the point of the bat he was in his glory; and upon my life, their speed was as the speed of thought'. 'Silver Bill' once hit a ball at a match on Molesey Hurst in 1787 for which ten runs were scored. Like most of the great cricketers of the eighteenth century he lived to an old age and died in 1862 aged 97. He had had two wives and thirty-nine children.

Several other clubs also used the ground as their headquarters. In 1769 the Knightsbridge Cricket Club, an exclusive club, 'only meant for Gentlemen Cricket players', advertised their 'Annual meeting at Moulsey Hurst being fixed for Saturday next, July 1st'.

In 1828 the Royal Clarence Cricket Club was formed under the patronage of the Duke of Clarence, who lived in Bushey Park. A contemporary report says: 'Moulsey Hurst is chosen as the headquarters of the club, and men are now actively engaged in levelling and laying down a suitable area of turf. The club will play every week during the season. Marquees will be pitched on the Hurst and lunches will be furnished'. Four years later 'The Royal Clarence Cricket Club has now to boast of between one and two hundred members, the major part of whom are entitled to be ranked as superior and scientific players of the game of cricket'. In spite of this proud boast, however, the club appears to have died out a few seasons later.

After the decline of the Royal Clarence Club little or no cricket was played on the Hurst until 1890, when the Hurst Park Racing Club was formed, and opened a cricket field in the centre of the racecourse. The pitch was enclosed and a change was made for admission. Some first-class matches were played there; even the touring Australian test team visited the ground, and were beaten by the club by 34 runs. However, the general attendance seems never to have been very high and the club folded up after a few years.

In 1758 the Hurst was the scene of yet another first, the first record of a game of golf to be played on English soil. Golf had, of course, been known in Scotland for centuries. The match was organised by David Garrick, who was entertaining a party of Scotsmen at Hampton, which included Rev Dr Carlyle, the minister of Iveresk, who wrote in his diary: 'Garrick had told us to bring clubs and balls, that we might play at golf on Moulsey Hurst. Garrick met us on the way, so impatient he seemed to be for his company. Immediately after we arrived, we crossed the river to the Golfing ground, which was very good'.

After the game the players sat on Garrick's lawn, where they were painted by Zoffany. The picture, which now hangs in Lambton Castle, shows clearly Molesey Hurst, the river, Tagg's Island, and the first Hampton Court bridge.

# Molesey Hurst Cricket Club - - 1/-
### at New Road, West Molesey.

Molesey Hurst C.C. v. B. Constable's Team

Sunday, September 13th 1959. Hours of Play: 11.30—6.0 p.m.

## IN AID OF B. CONSTABLE'S BENEFIT

**B. Constable's Team**
1. J. Edrich
2. T. H. Clark
3. M. J. Stewart
4. K. F. Barrington
*5. B. Constable
6. E. A. Bedser
‡7. R. Swetman
8. R. C. E. Pratt
9. D. Gibson
10. G. A. R. Lock
11. A. V. Bedser

**Molesey Hurst C.C.**
*1. C. Harding
‡2. R. Leighton
3. R. Cowley
4. A. Clapham
5. I. Duncan
6. J. Keeler
7. P. Newman
8. R. F. Peacock
9. A. Willoughby
10. J. Miller
11. E. Freeman
12. E. Knowlson
13. L. De Haviland
14. P. Holmes
15. M. Tate
16 E. Burchett

B , l-b , w , n-b

ABOVE: Molesey Hurst Cricket Club in the 1950s. Standing left to right: S. Willoughby (1st umpire), E. A. Bourne, H. Stenning (Team Sec.), A. G. Willoughby, J. Wheeler, E. Knowlson, M. S. Davenport, W. York, C. Harding, C. D. Mackie (Match Sec.), F. Boam, A. Brooker (Groundsman), F. W. Tate (2nd umpire). Sitting, left to right: R. F. Peacock (Treasurer), V. Rigby (2nd team Vice-Capt.), E. C. Turner (Captain), R. V. Peacock (2nd team Capt.), J. Wise (Chairman), P. Saywood (Vice-Chairman), A. Clapham (Vice-Captain), J. Blackwood, K. W. Tate. On Ground: P. York (Scorer). CENTRE: The Benefit match for B. Constable on 13 September 1959. BELOW: A zeppelin flies over Molesey Hurst golf course in 1930.

# *A Bloody Rendez-Vous*

Being close to town, yet sequestered enough to be undisturbed, 'the duel-stained sod of Moulsey Hurst', as Martin Tupper called it, was a favoured spot for 'affairs of honour'.

Perhaps the most famous duel to be fought here was one arranged between the fourth Earl of Tankerville, who lived at Mount Felix at Walton, and Mr Edward Bouverie, son of the Earl of Radnor. It seems that Mr Bouverie, a married man, took a house near the Earl's in order to pay attention to one of his five daughters. His lordship tried to warn him off and, when this failed to produce the desired effect, challenged him to an appointment on Mousley Hurst. They met at dawn on 1 July 1794 with their seconds, and took their stations at a distance of twelve paces. Mr Bouverie declined to fire, but the Earl had no such compunction. He pointed his pistol, took aim, pulled the trigger and wounded his opponent in the abdomen so severely that his life was endangered. In fact, his death was reported in *The Times*, which in the following week printed a retraction: 'We are happy to learn', they said, 'that the accounts which have been published in this and other newspapers, concerning the Hon. Mr. Bouverie, have been founded in error; so far that they announced his death. We are requested to state that Mr. Bouverie, though very severely wounded, is now in a fair way of recovery'. The seconds published a further announcement to the effect: 'We cannot omit our testimony of the coolness and good conduct displayed by both on this occasion'.

In 1810 a Captain Hants did not enjoy quite such good luck. His engagement on the Hurst produced such a dangerous wound that, although immediately moved to London, where a surgeon extracted the pistol ball from his left breast, he lingered and died in great pain after a few days. The *Gentleman's Magazine*, in reporting this event, says: 'He fell a dreadful sacrifice to a punctilious regard to those false principles of honour, which have so long, and so often, disgraced humanity. His antagonist has absconded'.

In fact there seems to have been a deliberate cover-up in high places to shield the antagonist, whose name was Coleshall. Although his identity was widely known, in fact he was even named in *The Times*, it was never mentioned at the coroner's inquest, and the jury was merely told 'that four gentlemen alighted from chaises on the Hurst, accompanied by another on horseback, and that two fires were exchanged, when the deceased fell, and was put in a chaise and driven off'. The verdict delivered was one of wilful murder against some person or persons unknown.

The sport (if such blood-lust really can be called sport) for which the Hurst achieved most contemporary renown, however, was prize-fighting. In the first two decades of the nineteenth century, when the Prince Regent and his bucks held sway, bare fist fighting was, according to Professor Trevelyn, 'the chief national interest', and more pugilistic encounters were settled on Molesey Hurst than in any other single place in England. Almost half of the recorded prize-fights between 1805 and 1824 were fought out on its turf. And what a scene it presented! From all corners of the country crowds came and poured onto 'the Pugilistic Waterloo', as it came to be called. Prints of the day show the ground packed tight with carts, coaches, horses, tents, and a milling throng of humanity, sometimes as many as ten thousand of them, all jostling for a place near the ringside. The scene was vividly described in the lines:

> 'To see the Hurst with tents encamped on,
> Look around the scene from Hampton.
> 'Tis life to cross the laden ferry,
> With boon companions wild and merry,
> And see the ring upon the Hurst,
> With carts encircled – Hear the burst,
> At distance of the eager crowd.
> Oh! it is life to see a proud
> And dauntless man step, full of hopes,
> Up to the P.R. stakes and ropes,
> Throw in his hat, and, with a spring,
> Get gallantly within the ring'.

Yet it was quite by accident that this ground came to such prominence. There had been one minor bout here back in 1797. Then, on Monday 11 March 1805, one Elias Spray, a coppersmith, was due to engage in fistic combat with Henry Pearce, nicknamed 'Hen' or 'The Game chickhen'; and Hampton was selected as the spot for the encounter. The Middlesex magistrates, however, had other views, for prize-fighting was illegal and, fearing an interruption from the authorities, the organisers decided to cross over into Surrey, where it seems the justices were thought to take their responsibilities in lighter fashion.

The *Morning Chronicle* says: 'Considerable confusion took place in procuring boats to convey the numerous followers across the river, where several not only experienced a good ducking, but some narrowly escaped drowning in their eagerness to reach the destined spot'. Another account described the scene: 'By hook or by crook the vast assemblage found themselves on the other side of the Thames and were on Moulsey Hurst, that place destined to see so many engagements in the ring afterwards. This occasion, however, was the very first time that the ropes and stakes were pitched upon that now classic spot; the most celebrated of trysting places connected with the prize ring'.

As the clock on the tower of Hampton Church struck one, the antagonists entered the ring and battered each other for thirty-five minutes and twenty-nine rounds, before Spray's seconds considered he had received enough punishment, and threw in the towel on his behalf.

The records of *The Ring* contain accounts of something like a hundred affrays which took place on the Hurst, and there were certianly dozens more of which reports never found their way into the journals.

Some of the pugilists who fought here were bestowed with the most enchanting of nicknames or *noms de guerre* – Alexander the Coalheaver, the Master of the Rolls (a baker by trade), the Streatham Youth, Holt the Duffer, the Chelsea Snob, the Phenomenon, Scroggins the Sailor, Dutch Sam, the Gaslight man.

The people who really profited whenever one of these fistic encounters took place were the ferrymen, the local innkeepers, and the toll collectors on the bridge. An expressive account tells us how the thousands rush to get home when the boats were over: 'The night fast approaching, the proverb of the "devil take the hindmost", seemed to be uppermost. The toddlers brushed off by thousands to the water's edge, and, in spite of the entreaties of the ferrymen, the first rush jumped into the boats in such numbers as nearly to endanger their own lives. However, the watermen soon got the best of it by demanding a bob or more to carry over in safety select companies. Yet so great was the pressure of the crowd, and so eager to cross the water to Hampton, that several embraced Old Father Thames against their will, amidst the jeers and shouts of their more fortunate companions. A nice treat, by way of a cooler, in an afternoon in November, sixteen miles distant from home. The other side of the Hurst produced as much fun and laughter, from the barouches, rattlers, gigs, heavy drags, etc., gallopping off towards Kingston Bridge through fields covered with water to save time. Several were seen sticking fast in the mud, the proprietors begging assistance from those persons whose horses were strong enough for the purpose. One block up of this kind operated on a string of carriages upwards of half a mile in length. The vehicles were so numerous, that two hours had elapsed before the whole of them had passed over Kingston Bridge, to the great joy and profit of the proprietors of the gates. For miles around Moulsey Hurst it proved a profitable day for the inns; and money that otherwise might have remained idle in the pockets of persons who could afford to spend it, was set to work in the consumption of articles tending to benefit hundreds of tradesmen, who otherwise might have been on the lookout for a customer'.

The greed of the ferrymen was the cause of at least one prize fight being lost to Molesey. It happened in June 1819, when Tom Shelton, 'The Navigator', was due to 'have a mill' with Ben Burn. The local ferrymen, who had a legal monopoly of the ferry across from the Hurst to Hampton, refused to share their pickings with the London watermen, and would not let them take people across the river. In fact, at a previous bout they had had several of them fined for so doing, whereupon the metropolitan men had their revenge by laying information before the magistrates that a fight was going to take place. This spoiled Molesey as a venue for the mêlée and Hounslow Heath was substituted, thereby denying to the ferrymen rich reward they undoubtedly would otherwise have reaped.

The end of the Hurst's flirtation with prize fighting came swiftly and decisively. By the mid 1820s the golden age of the Regency era had passed away. The affluent upper classes had withdrawn their support, and with it the rich purses they had lavishly contributed. The ring was taken over by sordid entrepreneurs, and corruption and bribery became rife. Without the countenance of Royal and aristocratic patrons, local magistrates were able to take positive action against the competitors and those who encouraged them.

In 1824 two pugilists, named Jem Burns and Ned Neale, pummelled each other on the Hurst, and were prosecuted for a breach of the peace. At Kingston Assizes Mr Justice Burroughs proclaimed that prize-fighting was contrary to the laws of the country, to be mercenary in origin, made up for the purpose of indulging the propensities of the vicious and encouraging the betting of the gamblers.

This judgement tolled the death-knell not only of fisticuffs on the Hurst, but of bare-knuckle fighting in general. For, as one writer has put it, 'the end of Moulsey precipitated the end of the prize ring. Many more fights took place but it was never again to enjoy the wide measure of patronage it had enjoyed in its Regency heyday'. Soon afterwards it could be said 'Now that the glory of pugilism is departed Moulsey Hurst has become a lonely place, it is a quiet spot enough, and void of offence'.

ABOVE: Dutch Sam fought Medley for 200 guineas on 31 May 1810 at Molesey Hurst.
BELOW: Thomas Cribb, England champion in 1808, gave a display at the Hurst with Bob Gregson, for a 1,000 guinea purse and the championship.

# Hampton Races

The extinction of prize-fighting did not leave Molesey Hurst entirely bereft of sporting encounters. On two days a year at least it sprang into life again as teeming masses thronged onto its turf for the annual carnival known as Hampton races.

Horses had been raced on the Hurst since the early seventeen hundreds at least, probably due, like so many other sports here, to the proximity of Hampton Court and the luxuried idlers it encouraged. But the meeting did not achieve much prominence until after the commencement of the next century. In fact, its renaissance may well have been influenced by the patronage of the sporting Duke of Clarence and his brood of illegitimate Fitzclarences from Bushy House just across the river. Even after his accession as William IV he continued his support and in 1831 donated a plate of one hundred guineas for a race run here.

The meeting, which was held in June each year, became more and more a festival for the plebeian masses of London. By the middle of the nineteenth century the gathering was estimated to attract over one hundred thousand souls on each day. Getting such a multitude on and off the Hurst was in itself a miraculous exercise, bringing difficulties and chaos to all the surrounding districts. The *Surrey Comet* commented: 'So great was the traffic through Kingston that it completely threw the Derby day into the shade'. And this was beside the shoals who came down on the special trains which were run from Waterloo, or travelled more leisurely by river steamer. No wonder the meeting was known as 'the Cockney Derby'.

Of all the race meetings held in the Kingdom this was pre-eminently the one at which the issue of the races paled into almost complete insignificance beside the collective enjoyment of the day's outing. Thus was it proclaimed by one newspaper 'of the thousands who frequent Molesey Hurst comparatively few care a fig which horse wins. They are out for the day, fixing upon one of two days of the meeting, because it is the thing to do. The staked-off course, stands, booths, and caterers for the pleasure and amusement of the people, give to the gathering rather the resemblance of a fair. The titled patrons of the turf were represented by several scions of noble houses, but it is for "the people" that Hampton draws its chief supply of visitors. The fun at times waxed exceedingly boisterous. The disregard for the racing in the minds of the majority was plainly shown in the difficulty experienced by the police in clearing the course for the first race, the holiday makers steadily refusing to be tempted from between the ropes'.

The scene has been vividly portrayed by the witty pen of perhaps the most observant and descriptive of our English novelists – Charles Dickens, in *Nicholas Nickleby*. 'The little race-course at Hampton was in the full tide and height of its gaiety; the day as dazzling as day could be; the sun high in the cloudless sky, and shining in its fullest splendour. Every gaudy colour that fluttered in the air from carriage seat and garish tent top shone out in its gaudiest hues. Old dingy flags grew new again, faded gilding was re-burnished, stained rotten canvas looked a snowy white, the very beggar's rags were freshened up, and sentiment quite forgot its charity in its fervent admiration of poverty so picturesque.'

'The great race of the day had just been run; and the close lines of people, on either side of the course, suddenly breaking up and pouring into it, imparted a new liveliness to the scene, which was again all busy movement. Some hurried eagerly to catch a glimpse of the winning horse; others darted to and fro, searching, no less eagerly, for the carriages they had left in quest of better stations. Here a little knot gathered round a pea and thimble table to watch the plucking of some unhappy greenhorn; and there, another proprietor with his confederates in various disguises, sought, by loud and noisy talk and pretended play, to entrap some unwary customer. These would be hanging on the outskirts of a wide circle of people assembled round some itinerant juggler, opposed in his turn, by a noisy band of music, or the classic game of "Ring the Bull", while ventriloquists holding dialogues with wooden dolls, and fortune-telling women smothering the cries of real babies, divided with them, and many more, the general attention of the company. Drinking tents were full, glasses began to clink in carriages, hampers to be unpacked, tempting provisions to be set forth, knives and forks to rattle, champagne corks to fly, eyes to brighten that were not dull before, and pickpockets to count their gains during the last heat. The attention so recently strained on one object of interest, was now divided among a hundred; and look where you would, there was a motley assemblage of feasting, laughing, talking, begging, gambling and mummery.'

'Of the gambling booths there was a plentiful show, flourishing in all the splendour of carpeted ground, striped hangings, crimson cloth, pinnacled roofs, geranium pots, and livery servants. There were the Strangers' club-house, the Atheneum club-house, the Hampton club-house, the Saint James's club-house, half a mile of club-houses to play in; and there were rouge-et-noir, French hazard, and other games to play at'.

The rows of refreshment booths, drinking tents, gingerbread stalls, shooting galleries, merry-go-rounds, and the like, imparted the appearance rather of an old-fashioned country fair – which was virtually what it was. And all this entertainment and catering was conducted by itinerant showmen, strolling gipsies, hawkers, and dealers, for whom the gathering was just as much a holiday mecca as for the patrons who were soon to be parted from their hard-earned cash.

For a week or more before the meeting the Hurst was asparkle as the travelling folk mustered, with their caravans, tents, camp-fires, their horses, barking dogs, clucking fowls, and lively, excited children. It appears that this place was liked by them much better than any other on their rambling itinerary. It was usually whilst staying here that advantage was taken to carry the year's offsprings along to West Molesey Church to be baptised. For many years after 1839 the parish register records each June, a list of 'travellers' and 'licensed hawkers' who had presented their babes at the font.

The gipsies, according to one report, 'were wonderfully well-behaved, and complaints of their behaviour were few and far between'. It was also noticeable that they departed much cleaner and more presentable than when they came. The same could not be said of some of the hangers-on who congregated around, and whose drunken orgies, for two or three nights, kept the neighbourhood in one continuous state of uproar and excitement.

The gipsy fraternity was composed of several close-knit families; the Sampsons, Lees and Rossitors being perhaps the most prominent, and amongst whom a conspicuous rivalry was forever manifest, especially between the latter two. This rivalry was usually evidenced only in amicable competition to outvie each other in the display of finery and trinkets, the flaunting of which was always a partiality of the romany.

However, on one notable occasion the rivalry broke out into bitter hostility and open fighting. This deadly struggle, which is faithfully retold by 'Lord' George Sanger, in his autobiography *Seventy Years a Showman*, came to a head at Molesey, when the two factions fought it out in a grand battle, using the large sticks, known as 'livetts', which were normally employed on the shies before wooden balls came into use. The combat was going famously, with neither side seeming to gain the advantage, when suddenly there arose a mighty roar as a posse of the local constabulary arrived to put a stop to the brawl. All at once the antagonism between the gipsies was forgotten and both parties turned as one, with brutal ferocity, on the blue uniforms, and a terrible struggle ensued. The police, who were few in number, were beaten mercilessly and were retreating towards the ferry when, with startling suddenness, the attacking gipsies ceased their mêlée and, as if a signal had been given, scampered to their various camps, which were immediately folded up, loaded onto carts, horsed-up, and they were away from the Hurst as fast as could be. Minutes later a strong reinforcement of armed police arrived on the scene, some arrests were made and it is believed that at least one of the Lees was imprisoned for his part in the contest. For many years afterwards the battle between the Lees and the Rossitors on Molesey Hurst was a talking point wherever the 'travelling folk' foregathered.

The massing of so many people onto the Hurst inevitably offered a field-day for a horde of criminal types, on the look-out for easy pickings from the gullible and unwary.

On the morning after the races a motley crowd of pickpockets, swindlers, gamblers, pilferers, and others engaged in unlawful acts, were presented at Kingston magistrates' courts, and were fined or sent away to enjoy the hospitality of one of HM's places of confinement for sundry spells. In 1859, for instance, four prisoners were sentenced to three months for picking pockets; five to one month each for stealing handkerchiefs; three boys to two months with hard labour for attempting to pick pockets; one charged with gambling with cards, case dismissed; one to hard labour for three months for stealing a shawl; a woman to three months for picking pockets; three were committed to sessions for assault and stealing; and one to three months' imprisonment for attempting to steal a gold watch and chain.

In 1866 an experiment was tried, by holding an additional meeting in the autumn, which proved so successful that it became an annual September feature. But this was a very different affair, with none of the razzle-dazzle of the June event, and the attendances nowhere near prolific. It was more for the racing types, where showmen and gipsies gave pride of place to bookmakers and tic-tac men. Some of the bookies, it was known, much regretted the proximity of Father Thames, for many a member of the fraternity who attempted to 'Welsh' on his clients 'had an involuntary ducking, sometimes with narrow escape from drowning, owing to inability to meet his betting liabilities'.

In 1881 the Prince of Wales attended the June meeting 'and if ever man enjoyed the fun of the fair', one writer tells us, 'it was he. His likeness was taken by an itinerant photographer, he had his fortune told, bought puppy dogs, and was as merry as every costermonger Joe from Whitechapel on his, perhaps, solitary day's outing during the year could have been'.

Being an open course there were few means available to the promoters of the races for the raising of sufficient money to defray the cost of upkeep, and little was done towards its maintenance. Indeed, it would have been uneconomic to expend a lot of money on a ground only used for racing on four days in each year. The course, therefore, deteriorated to a dilapidated condition, and in 1887 the Jockey Club refused to renew its licence, on the plea that it was unfit, if not positively dangerous, for racing. The meeting of that year saw the end of an era as far as 'Happy Hampton' was concerned.

ABOVE: Hampton Races – the ferry, Molesey 1866. BELOW: The crowds at Hampton Races, OPPOSITE: in 1821.

120

# HAMPTON RACES, 1821;

**KINGSTON LIST OF**  **PRINTED BY PERMISSION.**

FIRST DAY; WEDNESDAY, the 4th of JUNE,

## The Clarence Stakes of 5gs.

each, with 20gs. added from the Race-fund, for horses of all ages; the winner to be sold for 200gs. if demanded, three yr olds, 7st. four, 8st. 4lb. five, 9st. six and aged, 9st. 5lb. mares and geldings allowed 3lb. heats once and a half round the Course.—*Six Subscribers or no race.*

## A Purse of 100gs.

by subscribers of 5gs. each, the rest made up from the fund, for horses of all ages; three yr olds, 6st. 7lb. four, 8st. 2lb. five, 8st. 10lb. six and aged, 9st. mares and geldings allowed 3lb. the winner of any cup, plate or sweepstakes, to carry for once, 3lb. twice, 5lb. and thrice, 7lb. extra; the winner to be sold for 400gs. if demanded, &c. heats, once and a half round the Course.—*Five Subscribers or no race.*

SECOND DAY; THURSDAY the 5th.

## THE COBOURG STAKES OF 5gs. each,

with 20gs. added from the Race-fund, for horses of all ages; three yr olds, 6st. 5lb. four, 7st. 12lb. five, 8st. 7lb. six, 8st. 12lb. and aged, 9st. horses that have won once in 1821, to carry 3lb. extra, if twice, 5lb. and if three times, 7lb. extra; heats once and half round the Course.—*Five Subscribers or no race.*

## The Ladies' Plate of Fifty Guineas,

by a subscription of 5gs. each, the rest from the Race-fund; three yr olds, 6st. 4lb. four, 8st. 2lb. five, 8st. 12lb. six and aged, 9st. 3lb. mares and geldings allowed 3lb. the winner to be sold for 150gs. if demanded, &c. heats, once and a half round the Course; horses that have won in 1821, to carry for winning as for the Cobourg Stakes.—*Five Subscribers or no race.*

THIRD DAY; FRIDAY, the 6th.

## A SWEEPSTAKES of 20gs. each,

15gs. ft. for two yr old colts, 8st. 4lb. fillies 8st. 1lb. the new straight half mile.

## A Sweepstakes of 10gs. each,

for horses not thorough-bred, 11st. each; entire horses 3lb. extra; one-mile heats; Gentlemen riders.—Any horse having won once, to carry 5lb. extra, twice, 7lb. and three times, 10lb.—*Five Subscribers or no race.*

The horses to name for the Purse, Plate, the Cobourg, Clarence, and 10g. Sweepstakes Stakes, at the RED LION-INN, HAMPTON, on Saturday, the 30th, of June, between the hours of 4 and 7, with proper certificates, &c.

PRESENT SUBSCRIBER .................. Mr. SHAW.

Capt. FITZCLARENCE,  } STEWARDS.
Hon. Mr. WATSON,

JOSEPH FARRALL, Clerk of the Course.

[J. FRICKER, PRINTER, KINGSTON.]

121

ABOVE: The old stands, Molesey Hurst, John Taylor up. BELOW: The main stands.

# Hurst Park

After the closure of the old race-course the district was rife with speculation as to the future use of the site. The land was on lease to Mr John Taylor, of Manor Farm, West Molesey, but was owned by absentee lords of the manor; and it was the generally held opinion that they would immediately sell the estate for housing development.

However, a group of wealthy investors, who saw potential for the formation of one of the new 'park' type race-courses, banded together to form a syndicate to acquire the land and so to lay it out.

The interests of this company were more speculative than sportive. They had invested money with the object of making a profit and, if capital had to be spent on bringing the ground up to racing standards, patrons would have to pay to attend the meetings. No longer would the course be open to all and sundry. This meant, of course, enclosing the whole site within a fence, a requirement which was partially obstructed by virtue of an old road, originally running directly from the village of West Molesey to Hampton Ferry, the lower end of which had been diverted many years before the 'New Road' had been substituted; the upper end still traversed diagonally across the Hurst.

Application was made to West Molesey Parish Vestry – which was at that time the authority for local government in the area – for permission to divert the road to a different alignment. The request was backed up with the threat that, if such sanction was not forthcoming, there would be no race-course, and if there was no race-course the land would be sold for housing. Faced with such intimidation the parish had little choice but to allow the change to take place. At a vestry meeting held on 14 February 1889, with the Vicar, Rev T.G. Nicholas, in the chair, authority was granted to 'divert, stop-up, and turn' the old road, and to substitute a new carriageway of the width of forty feet and a length of about two thousand six hundred feet. This is, of course, the present Ferry Road, although it has since been truncated by posts erected across the road by the towpath.

There were some protests against the stopping-up of the old road, mainly from certain gentlemen living in East Molesey who had lost their short cut across the Hurst to the ferry; but the action was defended on the ground that the estate would be 'utilised in a manner that will at any rate preserve it from spoliation at the hands of the jerry builder'.

During the next few months gangs of workmen arrived on the Hurst, laying down the new road, levelling the site, constructing the stands, stables, and rings, raising the fence, and supplying 'every convenience for sporting purposes'.

It was this huge, all encompassing fence, seven feet high of close-boarded timber tarred over, which caused the most consternation. The residents of Hampton were particularly outraged that the view from Bell Hill, which previously had a pleasant prospect over the open Hurst, was now blighted by this obnoxious palisade and the vast new stands and other buildings.

The course, which was to be called Hurst Park, was intended to be run as a club, similar to the other park-type courses first started at Sandown in 1875. With a Members' Enclosure, access to which was restricted to members of the club and their properly vetted friends only, others would be restricted to the public stands and park.

However, the enterprise was not to be limited to horse racing only, but was intended to be a grand, general recreative venture, a sort of country club, to which end they also purchased the old mansion known as Hurst House, which stood in about sixteen acres of its own grounds, adjacent to the Hurst, on the corner of Hurst and New Roads, and which had been unoccupied for some seventeen years. As can well be imagined the house was then in a much run-down and dilapidated condition, and considerable capital had to be expended on bringing the building up to the state required for service as a private club-house. Stables were erected in the grounds for the accommodation of those members who preferred to drive down in their own carriages, and a dock, or marina as it would now be called, was cut from the Thames for the benefit of those who favoured the more leisurely journey by river.

It was intended, in fact, to be somewhat similar to Tagg's Club, with the added attraction of racing thrown in. The races were to be not only with the horses but with ponies, galloways, and trotting as well. Other sports were to be catered for by the laying down of polo grounds, tennis courts, and a cricket pitch, and the club-house was to be kept open for the delectation of members at all times. By January 1890 it was reported that the club had upwards of one thousand six hundred members, and that the club-house would be opened in a week or two.

As the race-course itself was rather short, being only a little over half-a-mile in length (the original Hurst, it must be remembered, lay only in West Molesey parish, and finished opposite the end of Hurst Lane), all the races had to be run over a round course; in default of a long, straight, sprinting run the Jockey Club would not issue a licence for flat racing. It was intended, therefore, to provide only hurdling and steeplechases for horses, and pony and galloway races outside the jumping season.

The course was opened for the first national hunt meeting on 19 March 1890, amid hails of great excitement. *The Times* newspaper declaimed: 'At present few even of its most constant habitues would recognise in Hurst Park the old Hampton racecourse and meadow, so completely have the aspects and surroundings been changed and beautified under the supervision of the Hurst Park club'.

The *Surrey Comet* told a similar story: 'On Wednesday morning, East Molesey and Hampton Court awoke to a scene of bustle and excitement, which recalled the long-faded glories of 'Appy 'Ampton, where the London coster and his friends abandoned themselves to the pleasures of the turf and periodical race meetings on the old Hurst. The occasion of this unwonted activity was the inaugural fixture of the Hurst Park Club. Amongst the earliest arrivals were race horses and a strong body of police. Seven special trains brought their freights of sporting men from Waterloo to Hampton Court Station, and two specials were reserved for members of the club. It is computed that over 2,000 people arrived by these trains. Large numbers of the patrons of the turf, however, preferred to travel by road. City omnibuses well laden arrived at intervals, and the familiar hansom, together with a continual stream of private conveyances and carriages of all descriptions, poured in their contribution from all parts'.

The first in what was anticipated to be a long run of pony meetings was held a month later, but the hopes of the promoters came nowhere towards fulfilment. Pony racing did not draw the crowds – they just stayed away.

In the event the whole enterprise turned rapidly into one vast belly-flop. There were losses on all later meetings except one – and that made a net profit of but £28 6s 11d. The total cost of setting up the club and laying out the course had amounted to nearly thirty-nine thousand pounds, the lease costing nine hundred pounds a year, and the deficiency on the first twelve months' trading reached almost two thousand three hundred pounds.

The cricket ground, it is true, had been opened in September 1890 with a much heralded match between the club, fortified by the addition of some well-known cricketing names, and the visiting Australian Test Team. It was complained that the pitch was not quite ready, and not up to the standard expected for first-class play. 'A fair company witnessed the day's play', but it was far too late in the season for this to have any effect on the overall financial fortunes of the club.

It was decided, therefore, to give up the pony and galloway racing as a dismal failure, and the social club had no hope of success without the racing, as it was seldom used except during meetings.

The only hope of retrieving the diminishing situation lay in procuring extra land, over and above the ninety-three acres of the old Hurst already held, to lengthen the course, in the expectancy of receiving a licence to hold flat-race meetings, and to present a good programme, with prizes sufficient to attract high-class fields, and trust thereby to break into the existing calendar.

Negotiations were concluded with Mr Kent to acquire a number of meadows at the eastern end, between the Hurst and Molesey Lock, on a twenty-one year lease at a rent of four hundred pounds per annum. These were levelled and laid out as a straight 'mile' course (although in fact, it was only seven furlongs), and new turnstiles were added.

The necessary licence was successfully obtained and flat racing commenced on 25 March in 1891, after which, for the next seventy-two years – except for the hiatuses of two world wars – success came and fortune flourished, so much so that in three years the syndicate were able to purchase the freehold at a cost of some seventy-five thousand pounds. The capital for that was raised by the issue of four per cent debenture stock, in one pound shares.

Hurst Park burst fitfully into international prominence in June 1913, as the scene of one of the more outrageous exploits of the women's suffrage movement. The 'Votes for Women' campaign, which had gained an ever increasing tempo, had by this time reached a crescendo of open warfare, culminating in an eruption of window-smashing, incendiarism, and destruction of public and private property of all kinds.

During the running of that year's Derby, Mrs Emily Davidson had tried to unseat the jockey from the King's horse, an attempt which had caused her to be badly trampled beneath the beast's hooves, and to receive such gruesome injuries that she died the following Sunday, 8 June.

The fatal news soon spread, and the authorities expected some sort of holy war of attrition to take place, but probably never anticipated a reaction either so swift or so violent.

Shortly after midnight a passing constable on cycle patrol along Hurst Road observed a glow emanating from near the grandstand, which almost immediately burst into a mass of flames. The Molesey Fire Brigade was summoned, and arrived with its steam pump within a few minutes, by which time the buildings, being constructed mainly of timber, were well engulfed in the blaze. Before long, neighbouring brigades also arrived – Kingston, Surbiton, Hampton, Hampton Hill and the Metropolitan Water Board. At one time the flames reached such a height that they could be seen as far away as Carshalton, and it lit the sky there so brilliantly that the local fire brigade turned out thinking the blaze was in their own district.

The firemen played the flames for some three hectic hours, pumping water from the Thames, before the conflagration was finally subdued. Came the daylight and the damage could be fully assessed. The main stand ended as 'a fantastic medley of charred wood, twisted iron, broken and melted glass, and gaunt fire-scorched pillars of brick'. The other buildings gutted included the member's and Tattershall's stands, the kitchens and dining rooms.

The initial cause of the blaze was soon established when a placard proclaiming 'Give the Women the franchise', and a quantity of suffragette literature were discovered.

Shortly afterwards two ladies were arrested at Richmond, and were charged before the magistrates at Kingston with being concerned together in feloniously and maliciously setting fire to the buildings and causing damage to the extent of £7,000. They were Clara Giveen (aged 26), a woman of independent means, and Kitty Marion (35), a music hall artiste. Both had seen the inside of prison before.

Of these two ladies, undoubtedly Kitty Marion is the better known. The younger girl, although an organiser for the Womens Political and Social Union, seems to have been shielded from some of the rigours of prison convictions by the efforts of influential friends.

Miss Marion, however, came from a much different background, and was much differently treated by the authorities. She had been born in Germany, but came to Britain to escape a tyrannous father, and joined the theatrical profession, treading usually on the boards of provincial music halls and variety theatre. She appears to have been as passionate and impulsive as her mop of violent red hair would betoken. Having been imprisoned as early as 1909 for breaking windows in Newcastle when Lloyd George went to visit Tyneside, she went on hunger strike, and resisted forcible feeding with intense vigour. Barricading her cell door with furniture, she kept the staff at bay until the next day when they managed to chisel the hinges away. On another occasion, when all metal objects had been removed from her reach, she broke open the pillow with her teeth, scattered the contents around, tore up the prison bible, and in the middle of the night, by breaking the glass of the gaslight, managed to set fire to the accumulation. By the time the smouldering combustion was detected and dowsed, the inmate was already in an insensible condition, and in her already weak state, was stimulated only after the employment of much effort.

At the opening of the Welsh National Eisteddfod in 1911, with some colleagues, she again tried to interrupt Lloyd George, but was roughly thrown out by the stewards, and set upon by the crowds, who fell on them, tore off their clothes, and snatched out lumps of hair. 'Being thrown to wild beasts', she afterwards declared, 'is nothing to being thrown to an infuriated mob. The former may tear you to pieces, but would draw the line at indecent assault'.

The two were committed to appear at the Surrey Assizes at Guildford, found guilty, and each sentenced to three years' penal servitude.

Of Clara Giveen little seems to have been heard of since, but Kitty Marion still kept her name and her cause in the public eye. She immediately went on hunger strike and, because of her weak condition, was released under the terms of the so-called 'Cat and Mouse Act'. She went straight round to the Home Office and threw a stone through a window, in protest at her release, for which she was again arrested, again sent to prison, again refused to eat, again released, and in an emaciated state taken to a nursing home. After serving four and a half months of her sentence she was finally discharged.

By this time rumblings of war with Germany were being heard and, because of her teutonic origins, Miss Marion decided to emigrate and went to live in the United States, where she eventually took American citizenship.

Such a fiery personality could not, of course, exist without giving her support to some under-dog and well-deserved undertaking so, still in the forefront of women's liberation, she threw herself into the birth control movement. Once again she was in the van of a crusading protest. For thirteen years she stood every day on the streets of midtown New York selling birth control literature, facing countless jeers with typical defiance and equanimity, and again being arrested many times. When the work came to an end in 1930 the American Birth Control League presented her with a cheque for five hundred dollars, and gave a grand luncheon in the Town Hall in her honour. She finally died in 1944.

The self-same war clouds which sent Kitty Marion scurrying off to America also brought changes to Hurst Park. The fire-ravaged stands were hastily rebuilt, but hostilities meant the cessation of racing for the duration. The park, however, fulfilled its duty in the service of the nation, as a training airfield for the Royal Flying Corps and the nascent RAF. It was again to house troops, both British and American, during the second struggle some twenty-five years later.

During the inter-war years and afterwards many improvements were made to the course and its facilities. The old Tattershall's stand was demolished, and replaced by a magnificent new one at a cost of £35,000; totalisators were added (among the first in the country), and photo-finish equipment installed, making Hurst Park not only one of the most up-to-date but one of the most intimate and friendly courses in the kingdom. As many as 50,000 individuals swarmed down (principally by the special trains – four shillings return including entrance to the course) on Whit-Monday, the most popular meeting in the calendar.

By 1960 rumours began to circulate that the end of Hurst Park was in sight. It was still a popular venue, meetings were well attended, and it was making a profit. But for the proprietors it was a business venture, and more money was to be obtained from property development than from horse racing, so the blow was struck. Application was made to build houses on the site and, in spite of a spirited opposition put up by Molesey people, planning permission was granted.

On Wednesday 10 October 1962, at 4.30 pm, a chesnut named Anassa, the favourite at 11–8, won the Byfleet Stakes, the last race ever to be run on this once classic course. One London bookmaker (and bookies are not normally noted for sentimentality), hung a funeral wreath of chrysanthemums around the winning post, bearing a card with the simple message: 'With sincere memories of a friendly racecourse from all racegoers'. The donor bemoaned: 'This is a sad day for me. Mind you I've never won much money – here as elsewhere – but it was such a happy course'.

Happy course or not, in the sacred fulfilment of producing the most profit for its shareholders, it had to go. Soon the auctioneer started to bang his gavel; acres of the verdant turf – noted for its springiness over a hundred and fifty years before – was knocked down to Royal Ascot; the largest stand – over 95 yards long – went to Mansfield Town Football Club, and the railings to a dog track. Everything from starting gates to park benches, number boards to paving stones, the fire engine to ladies' loos; altogether some six hundred and sixty-five lots were sold to the highest bidder, bringing in about ten thousand pounds. Thus ended the centuries' long sportive associations of Molesey Hurst.

ABOVE: Horses leave the paddock at Hurst Park. CENTRE: The Royal box and grandstand, after the suffragette arson attack, June 1913. RIGHT: Kitty Marion of the women's movement.

An Act to provide for the closing of part of Ferry Road in the urban district of Esher in the county of Surrey during the Hurst Park races and for closing a footpath and for other purposes.

[26th April 1949.]

WHEREAS in order to effect improvements in the Hurst Park Race Course it is expedient to construct an extension of the course which will cross Ferry Road in the urban district of Esher in the county of Surrey (which road is a highway not repairable by the inhabitants at large) and it is expedient to make provision for the closing of part of that road on the days on which races are held at Hurst Park:

And whereas it has been alleged that there was a public footpath across Hurst Park extending from the southerly side of the towing path at Hampton Ferry in a southerly direction to a point in Hurst Road approximately four hundred and seventy-three yards from the junction of that road with Ferry Road but that footpath (if it existed) has not been used by the public for upwards of fifty years and for the removal of doubt it is expedient that the provisions of this Act in regard thereto should be enacted:

ABOVE: Sir Winston Churchill joins the members in their enclosure at Hurst Park. BELOW: The 1949 Act to close part of Ferry Road.

*Racecards not bearing this signature are spurious*

*P. M. Beckwith-Smith*

# HURST PARK

### OCTOBER MEETING, SECOND and FINAL DAY
(Under Rules of Racing)

## WEDNESDAY, 10th OCTOBER, 1962

**STEWARDS**
SIR HUMPHREY DE TRAFFORD, BT., M.C.
THE MARQUESS OF ABERGAVENNY, O.B.E.
THE HON. RICHARD STANLEY, M.P.
THE HON. J. P. PHILIPPS

**STEWARDS' SECRETARIES**
COMMANDER C. R. THOMPSON
BRIGADIER J. Le C. FOWLE

**OFFICIALS**
Handicapper—Mr. D. G. SHEPPARD   Starter—MAJOR P. W. CRIPPS
Judge—CAPT. V. D. BURTON
Clerk of the Scales—Mr. G. W. GREGORY
Veterinary Officer—LT.-COL. R. H. KNOWLES, M.R.C.V.S.
Medical Officer—DR. J. W. M. HUMBLE
Veterinary Surgeons—Mr. J. A. MORRIS, M.R.C.V.S. and Mr. A. G. LIMONT, M.R.C.V.S.
Auctioneer—Mr. G. S. FORBES
Stakeholders—MESSRS. WEATHERBY & SONS
Public Relations Officer—Mr. BRIAN GETHING
Club Secretary—Mr. R. V. HARGREAVES
Manager and Clerk of the Course—MAJOR P. M. BECKWITH-SMITH
Address—The Racing Stables, West Molesey, Surrey
Telephone—Molesey 364

**Official Programme**          **Price One Shilling**

Published by authority of the Clerk of the Course and
printed by Knapp, Drewett & Sons Ltd., Kingston-on-Thames

---

SIXTH RACE     One mile, five

**4.30—THE BYFLEET STAKES** of
and a further 2 sov. if forfeit be not declared
**three yrs old and upwards**; three yrs old
allowed 3lb; horses which have not won this
those which have not won such a race this y
not won such a race this year value 350 sov.
to receive 10% and the third 5% of the whole
4 sov. forfeit declared for 15, and 2 sov. for 32

VALUE TO THE WINNER £485 6s.; TO

3 **BROCADE SLIPPER** ...... Mr
   Ch h Solar Slipper—Brocade
4 **ROSOLIO** ............ Mrs J. M
   B g Fontenay—Rosamée
6 **TOBAGO** ................ L
   Ch g Borealis—Nassau
7 **RAPHAEL** ......... Sir Franc
   Br c Zucchero—Foxella
8 **WHERE'S MAMMA** .. Mr D.
   B m Mustang—Hallie
9 **ANASSA** ........... Mr B.
   Ch f Pardal—Janie Mou

LEFT: The last day's racing at Hurst Park – 10 October 1962 (and below, the last race). BELOW: Place your bets! RIGHT: A wreath for remembrance.

# HURST PARK RACE COURSE.
## MOLESEY, SURREY.

PRICE 1/-.

## CATALOGUE OF THE VALUABLE
# RACE COURSE EQUIPMENT

INCLUDING

RUNNING RAILS, FENCING, STARTING GATES, PHOTO FINISH TOWER, NAME & NUMBER BOARDS, TWO GRANDSTANDS, AUTOMATIC SPRINKLER SYSTEM, WEIGHING-IN SCALES, TURNSTILES, PORTABLE TIMBER BUILDINGS, FORDSON TRACTOR, GANG AND OTHER MOWERS, LAND ROVER, MASSIVE ENTRANCE GATES, PORTABLE PAINT SPRAYER, GARDEN SEATS, GAS FIRED BOILERS, THREE ROTA SCYTHES, MINIMAX FIRE ENGINE, FURNITURE AND EFFECTS, SAFES, TRAILER, KITCHEN & CATERING EQUIPMENT, FIXTURES & FITTINGS & USEFUL MISCELLANEA

**TO BE SOLD BY AUCTION ON THE COURSE**

## On TUESDAY, 6th NOVEMBER, 1962 AND DAY FOLLOWING.

COMMENCING AT 11 A.M. EACH DAY.

ON VIEW—SATURDAY & MONDAY, 3rd & 5th NOVEMBER, 1962, From 9 a.m.—4 p.m. ...ch Day.

...END GREEN & Co.,
...TORIA STREET,
...DON, S.W.1.
e Gallery 0088).

| LOT | |
|---|---|
| 424 | A 2ft 6in WALNUT REPRODUCTION DRESSING TABLE with frieze drawer, on cabriole legs and carved knees |
| 425 | A small modern easy chair with sprung seat and back, upholstered in floral chintz |
| 426 | A pair of heavily carved plant stands with rouge marble inset tops (slightly faulty) |
| 427 | A similar pair |
| 428 | Three odd ditto |
| 429 | Three ditto (taller) |
| 430 | Three Moorish coffee tables with inlaid mother-o'-pearl (all slightly faulty) |
| 431 | A set of 3 interlocking coffee tables with carved frieze and 2 inlaid rosewood top occasional tables |
| 432 | A SET OF EIGHT EARLY ENGLISH CHAIRS, comprising: Two elbow and six standard, with shaped splat backs and drop-in seats (some faulty) |

The sale of Hurst Park Racecourse equipment, 6/7 November 1962.

ABOVE: Hampton Church, 1860 and BELOW: at the turn of the century.

# Hampton Reach

'A place where Nature's choicest gifts adorn,
Where Thames' kind streams in gentle current turn,
The name of Hampton hath for ages borne.'

When permission was granted to allow building development on the Hurst, the planning authorities at least insisted that a wide strip of open grassland was to be left between the blocks of houses and Father Thames, creating a recreation area which is much appreciated by the hundreds who on any warm weekend may be seen picnicking, watching the craft on the river, or just lying on the grass sunning themselves. It is along this green expanse that our ramble now leads us.

This is one stretch of our walk which has definitely improved over the years, most particularly by the eradication of the old fence which formerly encircled Hurst Park, an infernal rampart which had been the target of remonstration ever since the day it was first erected.

In 1930 a town planning survey commissioned by the Middlesex and Surrey County Councils described the towpath here as uninteresting, 'owing to the high and ugly fence erected to withhold from the public the view of races taking place on Hurst Park Racecourse which occupies the river frontage for some considerable distance. The fence is substantially built in wood and keeps a uniformly ugly and undeviating line for over a mile. It is a graceless and forbidding protection of vested interests'. The report suggested that: 'The planting of tall growing poplars along the boundary of the fence would mitigate the sense of bareness and make a fine line of green'.

The surveyors did state, however, that the fence was 'innocent of any form of advertisements', something they could not have said even a few years before this, for it had been the custom on every race day to nail placards upon the fence all the way along the towpath and round Hurst Road as well. So many and so tightly packed together were they that barely a square foot of the original fence could be seen. Nobody ever took the trouble to remove them, the consequence of which, when time, rain and weather had all taken their toll, was a tattered and sorry mess all round.

At one time an even greater threat to the scenery here was mooted which, had it been carried out, would have been nothing short of an environmental disaster.

In 1858 plans were deposited with the clerk of the peace to seek Parliamentary sanction for the construction of a railway line to run from Twickenham, through Teddington, Hampton, West Molesey and East Molesey, to connect with the existing branch line at Hampton Court Station. This railway would have spanned the Thames on a massive, hideous bridge where we now stand, which would undoubtedly have ruined the riverscape for all time. Luckily for us the monstrosity was never erected, which may have been due to the tremendous capital outlay that such a viaduct would have entailed, plus the pressure which was exerted by the residents of Sunbury and Shepperton, who wanted the line to run to their district. Their wish was granted. Shepperton got the line instead. For such mercy we ought to be eternally grateful.

At this point the Thames broadens out to almost lake-like proportions and the water becomes alive, at week-ends, with white and blue sails, as the yachts tack and veer across the stream in a seemingly aimless saraband. And above all Hampton Church lords it over the scene like the chairman at a meeting.

Hampton's parish church, St Mary's, is a handsome structure in the Perpendicular style, dating from 1830, when it replaced the ancient temple which had stood here from medieval times, but had then become too small for the growing village. The main attraction of the present building lies in a number of historically interesting memorials and gravestones. Jerome's *Three Men in a Boat* were enjoined by Harris to stay a while here to 'go and see Mrs. Thomas's tomb'. He did not quite know who Mrs Thomas was, but 'She's a lady thats got a funny tomb, and I want to see it'.

During the winter of 1962/3, when the frost started on Boxing Day and hung around virtually continuously until the end of February, the river was frozen to a depth of a foot or more. Even the efforts of an ice-breaker failed to keep a navigation channel open.

> 'Famed Thames with shiv'ring winter dresses,
> With icicles and borrow'd tresses,
> And on her head a periwig of snow,
> And freezed mantle fring'd with ice below.'

Although no fair was held on the ice, as it was in the seventeenth century when the lines above were penned, a well wrapped-up humanity was scattered over the river, skating, snowballing or (like the present writer) just strolling, so that they could recount to generations not then born that they had walked across the Thames from West Molesey to Hampton in the great freeze-up of '63. Some foolhardy youths even managed to get a small motor car onto the ice, and drove it where normally the only conveyance was the public ferry.

And so, looking back at the frozen river of 1963, and recalling Pepys' words of three centuries before: '...a bitter cold frosty day, the frost being now grown old and the Thames covered with ice' we needs must leave the towpath, while looking forward to returning in the spring with William Morris: 'The clear Thames bordered by its gardens green,' and, in the knowledge that, as another year passes, we too become a small part of this splendid river's 'liquid 'istory'.

A delightful Edwardian day out, with the Church across the river.

ABOVE: Hampton Ferry and landing stage. BELOW: The great freeze-up of 1963.

# BIBLIOGRAPHY

Barrie, J. M. *My Lady Nicotine*
   *Walker London*
   *When A Man's Single*
Cobbett, Martin *Wayfaring Notions* (1906)
Derry, E. *Four Days on the Thames* (1899)
Dickens, Charles *Nicholas Nickleby*
Drayton, Michael *Poly-Olbion* (1622)
Hall, Samuel Carter & Anna Maria *The Rock of the Thames* (1869)
Jeffries, Richard *Open Air Book*
   *Native near London*
Jerome, Jerome K. *The Open Air* (1885)
   *Three Men in a Boat* (1889)
Jesse, Edward *Anglers' Rambles* (1836)
Law, Ernest *History of Hampton Court Palace* (1891)
Manning, Eliza F. *Delightful Thames* (1886)
Murray, John *Guide to Surrey* (1898)
Palmer, Joseph *A View of Hampton from Molesey Hurst* (1797)
Penwell, Joseph & Elizabeth *The Stream of Pleasure* (1891)
Ripley, Henry *History and Topography of Hampton on Thames* (1885)
Sanger, 'Lord' George *Seventy Years A Showman*
Spenser, Edmund *Prothalamion* (1596)
Wright, *English Dialect Dictionary*

# Index

Figures in *italics* refer to illustrations

AC Cars Ltd ............ 89,90,95
Adam, brothers ............ 103
   Robert ..................... 103
Alexander the
   Coalheaver ............. 114
Alexander,
   Beaumont ............. 87,88,91
Allen, Thomas
   Newland ................. 32,33
Allnut, Zachary .............. 39,40
American Birth
   Control League ............. 127
Anassa ........................... 127
Andrews, Herbert .............. 95
Anglers' Ait ..................... 53
Ash Island ............. 43,53,54
   59,65,66,107
Ashen Ait ....................... 53
Austin, Charles ................. 16
Australian Test Team ....... 125
Baker, PC Walter ............... 96
Barge Walk ................. *61,78*
Barrie, J.M. ........ 68,69,70,91
Bedster, W. ..................... 111
Beldham, William
   'Silver Billy' ............ *108*,111
Bell Hill ......................... 123
Bennett, Billy ................... 79
Block, H.A. ...................... *62*
   N. ................................. *62*
Boer War ......................... 72
Bouverie, Edward ............. 113
Bradford, John ............ 67,68,72
Bromfield, William ............ 38
Bronesky, Leon .................. 91
Brown, Capability ............ 103
Bundy, A.E. ................... 89,91
Burn, Ben ....................... 115
Burns, Jem ..................... 115
   John ............................. 11
   Tom .............................. 53
Burrell, Sir Peter .............. 111
Burrell-Burrell, A. ............. 71
Burroughs, Justice ........... 115
Bute, Lord ...................... 110
Byfleet Stakes ................ 127
Carlyle, Rev Dr ................ 111
Casino ............................ *91*
Cedars, The ..................... 97
*Chambers' Journal* ......... 110
Chaplin, Charlie ............ 79,90
   Sid ................................ 79
Charles II ........................ 97
Chelsea Snob, the ........... 114
Chippendale ................... 103
Churchill, Sir
   Winston ...................... *129*
Clarke, James ............... 21,22
Cigarette Island ....... 15,16,17
   *18*,21,40
Clarence, Duke of ....... 111,117
Clore, Charles ............... 89,91
Cobbett, Martin ........ 35,51,66
   William ......................... 51
Coleshall, Mr ................. 113
Constable, B. .................. *112*

Cory, Mrs ...................... *101*
   Theodore ................ 97,*101*
Cowdy, Mr ...................... 58
Cribb, Thomas ................ 116
Cyril, Herbert ............ 87,88,91
Daly, John ....................... 85
Davidson, Mrs ................ 125
Davis family .................. 15,52
Derry, E. ........................ 103
Dewar, Sir Thomas ............ 85
Dickens, Charles ......... 35,117
Drayton, Michael ............. 15
Duck Eyot ....................... *96*
Dutch Sam .............. 114,*116*
Egmont, Lord ................... 16
Eliot, T.S. ........................ 35
Elmbridge Borough
   Council ...................... 52,53
Ember, River ................. 15,22
Emney, Fred .................... 90
Esher UDC ...................... 17
Feltham estate ............. 35,*55*
Feltham, James ................ 34
Ferry House .................... 51
Flanagan and
   Allen ............................ 79
Foreman, Sir Henry .......... 16
Fred Karno's Army ........... 79
Garrick, David ........... 103,104
   *106*,111
   David jr ......................... 97
Garrick's Ait .................. 107
   Grotto ......................... *106*
   House .... *10*,64,97,*100*,*102*
   Island .................... *106*,107
   Lawn ................. 53,*101*,111
   Lower Eyot ................... 53
   Temple ................. 53,*62*,71
   Villa ...... *62*,97,103,104,*105*
Gaslight man, the ........... 114
*Gentleman's Magazine* .... 113
George III ...................... 110
George, Lloyd ................. 126
Gerrard, Gene .................. 79
Gilmour, J.L. .................... 68
Giveen, Clara ................. 126
Graburn, Lt Col
   'Willy' .......................... 95
Graham, Winifred ............. 97
Gregson, Bob .................. *116*
Grignion, C. ..................... *23*
Griggs Hill
   Green .......................... *36*
Gull, The ........................ *96*
Gwyn, Nell ...................... 97
Hall, Anna Maria .............. 11
   Samuel Carter ............... 11
Hambledon .................... 111
Hampton ....... 53,54,59,81,85,
   96,103,109,111
   114,115,124,
   125,133,134
   Church .......... *10*,23,40
   51,53,96,114,*132*,134,*135*
   Court ..... 11,15,21,34,37,40
   59,65,66,104,117,124

Bridge ................... 14,18
   21 *et seq*, 23,24,25,
   26,28,29,30,31,32,35,36
   40,41,46,53,66,111
   Palace ... *18*,22,40,51,109
   Deeps ......................... 97
   Ferry ....... *19*,*120*,123,*136*
   House ....................... 103
   Races ..... 117 *et seq*, *120*,*121*
   Reach ................ 133 *et seq*
   Station .............. *13*,124,133
   UDC ............................ 84
Hants, Captain ............... 113
Harvey, Joseph .... 53,54,66,91
Harvey's Ait ..................... 53
Hassell, E. ....................... *49*
Hawkes, Jerry ................... 52
Hawthorn,
   Nathaniel .................... 17
Hay, Will ......................... 79
Heckel, A. ........................ *23*
Henry VIII ....................... 17
Herbert Cyril & Co ............ 87
Hewitt, H. ................. 59,*73*,80
Higher Ait ................ 104,*106*
Hitler's War ..................... 33
Hodgson, Col ................... *36*
Hog Hole ......................... 65
Holmes, Oliver
   Wendell ..................... 107
Holt the Duffer ............... 114
Home Guard ................... 33
Houseboats
   Arcadia .................... 68,69
   Astoria ............... 80,*81*,*82*
   97,98,*101*,103
   Castle .......................... 16
   Cheznous ..................... 16
   Cigarette ..................... 16
   Cosy Corner ................. 81
   Gipsy ........ *10*,67,68,72,*75*
   Grantully Castle ........... 59
   Happy Days ................. 16
   Highland Lassie ........... 80
   Minosa ........................ 16
   Nirvana ....................... 16
   River Dream ................ *75*
   Satsuma ............... 59,*73*,80
   Shop Girl, The ............. 59
   Siesta .......................... 59
   Wildflower ................... 16
How, J. ........................... *26*
Howes, Bobby .................. 79
Hudd, Roy ....................... 90
Hurlock,
   William C. ............. 89,95,96
Hurst House ........ 97,111,123
   Park ... 21,22,33,52,57,71,86,
   94,95,107,123,*et seq*,128,
   129,130,131,133
   Club ...................... 107,124
   Racing Club ............... 111
Hurstside ....................... 59
Hylton, Jack ........ 84,88,94,98
Immisch Electric Launch
   Co Ltd .......................... *73*

Inns, Pubs and Hotels
   Albion Inn .................... 66
   Anglers' Retreat,
     The ................ 53,66,67,69
   Carnarvon Castle
     Hotel ..................... 33,59
   Casino Hotel ................. 89
   Castle Hotel ........... 26,28,29
   Inn ........... 14,15,22,33,59
   Ferryboat Inn ............... 33
   Island Hotel ........ 83,84,85,95
   Johsua Tree .................. 33
   Mitre Hotel ... 22,23,*28*,29,35
   Prince of Wales Hotel ...... 57
   Thames (Tagg's Thames)
     Hotel ............. *14*,*28*,*29*,32
     34,35,*36*,66,*76*,91
'Jail Birds' ....................... 79
Jeffries, Richard ......... 16,52,57
Jerome,
   Jerome K. ............. 37,69,134
Jesse, Edward .................. 66
Jewell, Jimmy .................. 90
Jockey Club ............... 119,124
Johnson, Dr ............... 103,104
   Jack ............................. 87
Kaiser's War ........... 16,95,104
Karno (Westcott),
   Fred ......... 79 *et seq, 82, 83*
   *et seq*, 90,91,*92*,97,98
   Fred jr .......................... 80
   Mrs ............................. *82*
Karsino .......... 53,84 *et seq*, 90,*92*,
   *93*,*94*,96
Kelsall, A.F. .................... 97
Kent, C.W. ............. 62,83,89,91
   family .......................... 83
   Francis Jackson ........ 65,72
   Mr ......................... 57,125
Kent's Ait ....................... 65
Kilfoyle, A. ....................... 58
Kingston ................. 109,117
   119,125,126
Kitchin, Fred ............... 16,79
Knightsbridge
   Cricket Club ................. 11
Knox, Isa Craig ................. 96
Laurel, Stan .................... 79
Law, Ernest ..................... 37
Lee family ................ 118,119
Lennox, Hon Col ............. 111
Lloyd, Marie .................... 16
Local Government Board ... 53
Lock, Mrs Hester .............. 65
London United Electric
   Tramway ..................... *36*
Long Ditton .................... 43
Ludgator, Benjamin ........ 21
Lupino, Barry .................. 79
Lutyens,
   Sir Edwin ......... 22,23,*31*,33
Lyons, Joe ....................... 81
Lytton, Henry A. .............. 81
Manning, Eliza F. .......... 34,44
Manor Farm ................... 123
Marion, Kitty ....... 126,127,*128*

Martin family ...................... 52
Master of the Rolls ........... 114
Matcham, Frank ................. 83
Mayo, Mr ............................ 33
McLachlan Mr .................. 107
McNaughton Brothers ....... 16
Medland, Mr ..................... *102*
Medley, Mr ....................... *116*
Melville, Jack ..................... 90
Metropolitan Board
  of Works .......................... 22
  Water Board .................... 43
Milbourn, Tom ................... *56*
Milbourne family ............... 52
Miller, Max ........................ 79
Milner, James Abram ........ 57
Mole, River ........ 15,22,51,107
Molesey ................................ *4*
  Band ........................... 35,59
  Bathing Station .............. 107
  Boat Club
    54,57,58,59,*61*,*62*,95
  Council ............................ 33
  Cricket Club ........ 57,95,*98*
  East ........ 11,21,38,65,66,83,
    96,123,124,133
  East and West UDC .... 17,52
  Fire Brigade ................... 125
  Hurst ..... 21,40,41,51,95,109,
    110,111,113,114,115,*116*,117,
    119,*122*,123,125
  Cricket Club
    .................. *108*,110,*112*
  Golf course .................... *112*
  Labour Party .................... 47
  Local Board ..................... 35
  Lock .... 3,*13*,*14*,34,37 et seq,
    45,*48*,*50*,51,52,53,79,125
  Lockhouse ................... 49,*55*
  Matham, Manor of ........ 109
  Mill ............................. 15,*26*
  Park .................................. 95
  Prior ............................ 21,33
  Weir .............. 49,*50*,*61*,97
  West ........ 10,11,21,65,*73*,95,97,
    104,107,109,123,124,133,134
  Church ........................... 118
  Parish Vestry ................. 123
*Morning Chronicle* ........... 114
Morris, William ........ 17,134
Mount Felix ............... 111,113
Mr Clay's Ait ................ 53,57
'Mumming Birds' .............. 79
Murray, E. T. ...................... 22
  John .................................. 11
Nash, John ........................ 41
Naughton and
  Gold ................................. 79
Noale, Ned ...................... 115
Nervo and Knox ............... 79
Nervo, Jimmy ................... 90

New Hampton Court Club,
  The ................................... 72
  Princes Restaurant ........... 87
*Nicholas Nickleby* ........... 117
Nicholas, Rev T. G. .......... 123
Nyron, John ..................... 111
Ogilvy, Gavin ..................... 68
O'Hagan, H. H. .................. 59
Old Walton Bridge ............. 40
Painshill, Cobham ........... 103
Palmer, Joseph ...... 96,104,109
Pandit, Ramsawak Doon .... 90
Peacock, Thomas Love ...... 67
Pearce, Henry .................. 114
Pearce-Brown, Charles ...... 87
Pennell, Elizabeth ......... 37,38
  Joseph ......................... 37,38
Pepys, Samuel ................. 134
Phenomenon, the ............ 114
Phillips, David .................. 42
Pig Hunt ........................... 58
Piper, A. ............................ *62*
Platts Ait ............. 40,59,*73*,80
Pope, Alexander ............... 17
Potterton, E. ...................... 71
Powell, Sandy ............... 79,90
Prince of Wales, Frederick
  Louis ........................ 109,110
RAF ................................. 127
Ray, J. ................................ 52
Regattas ......... 38,*61*,*62*,*63*,64
  Amateur ..................... 58,*60*
  Boat Club ....................... 58
  Invitation ........................ 58
  Watermen's and Fishermen's
    ....................................... 58
Rennie, John ..................... 40
Revnell, Ethel ................... 90
Reynolds, Rev W. F. .......... 95
Richard I. ........................... 39
Richmond Council ............ 90
*Ring, The* ....................... 114
Ripley, Anthony ................ 67
Riverholme ....................... 65
Roads and Streets
  Bridge Road ......... 40,52,66
  Cherry Orchard Road ... 109
  Creek Road .................. 15,52
  Feltham Avenue ............. 34
  Ferry Road .............. 123,*129*
  Graburn Way .............. 85,95
  Hampton Court Road ..... 97
  Way ............................ 15,22
  Hurst Lane ............... 109,124
  Road .......................... 40,96
    109,124,125,133
  New Road
    ................... 109,111,123,124
  Palace Road ............ 11,51,57
  Portsmouth Road ...... 22,103
  Summer Road .................. 17

Robinson Crusoe Island .... 53
Robinson, Lady ............... 104
  Sir Clifton ..................... 104
  W. P. ................................ 22
Rossitor family .......... 118,119
Roubiliac .................. 104,*106*
Rowlandson, Thomas ........ *25*
Royal Clarence Cricket Club
  ....................................... 111
  Flying Corps .............. 94,127
Russell, Billy ..................... 90
*Saint James's Evening Post* ... 109
St Albans ............. 97,*100*,*101*
Sampson family .............. 118
Sanger, Lord George ........ 118
Scroggings the Sailor ....... 114
Shakespeare, William
  (statue of) ............... 104,*106*
Shank's Ait ............... 104,*106*
Shelton, Tom .................. 115
Sheparde, Thomas ............ 21
Sheridan, Brinsley ............ 66
  Frank ............................. 66
Sisley, Alfred ................ 12,*14*
Smith, Jack ....................... 87
  W. H. ............................. 59
Spenser, Edmund .............. 12
Spray, Elias ..................... 113
Stapleton, John ...... 15,21,109
Steamers
  *Duke of York* ................. 13
  *King, The* ....................... 52
  *Marchioness* ................... 52
  *Viscountess* ..................... 52
Stede, Mr ........................ 110
Stevens, Edward 'Lumpy'
  .......................................111
  Samuel ............................ 21
Strathavon, Lord .............. 111
Streatham, Youth, the ...... 114
Sunbury Flats .................... 40
  Lock .................. 11,40,41,43
*Surrey Comet* ......... 35,38,57,58,
  71,72,84,86,88,96,117,124
Surrey Bn Home Guard ..... *36*
Swan's Nest Island ....... 96,97
Swiss Chalet ...................... *75*
Tagg, family ............ 52,74,91
  George John ...... 66,71,72,83
  Harry ..................... *32*,34,35
  John ................................ 66
  Sam ................................. 66
  Thomas ....................... 58,59
  Thomas George
    ................... 58,59,66,71,95
  Tagg's Club .................... 124
  Island ........... 53,54,59,65
    et seq,*75*,76,79,80,*81*,*82*,
    83 et seq,*91*,95,96,97,111
  Hotel Ltd ....................... 72
  Properties Ltd .............. 89

Tankerville, Lord ....... 111,113
Tappling, Richard .............. 58
Tate, Harry ........................ 16
Taylor, John .............. *122*,123
Teddington Lock ...... 15,40,43
Temple of Shakespeare
  ............................. *102*,104,*106*
Thames Angling Preservation
  Society ...................... 52,66
  Conservancy ...........35,39,42
    43,51,53,*55*,96,107
  Board ............................. 53
  Ditton ............. 17,37,66,89
  Motor Cruising Club ....... 23
  River ........ *10*,11,*12*,15,16,23
    37,38,39,41,51,52,53,*54*
    57,96,107,115,119,133,134
  Riviera ................... 88,89,*94*
  Valley Sailing Club .......... 59
Thorne, James .............. 15,23
Thornhill, Sir James ...... 15,*19*
Three Karnos, The ............. 79
*Times, The*
  ................53,83,89,90,113,124
Tom Tagg's Boat Clubhouse
  ....................................... 78
Tombleson, Mr .................. *26*
Town Hall ....................... 127
Trevelyn, Professor .......... 113
Tufton, Hon J. ................. 110
Tupper, Martin ................ 113
United Kingdom
  Advertising Co ................ 88
Upper Deck Swimming Pool
  ............................. 52,53,*54*
Venetian Fête .................... 59
Victoria, Queen ................. 16
Vesta ................................. 98
Walker, Sid ........................ 79
Walnut Tree Island ............ 65
Walton Bridge .................... 11
Walton-on-Thames .... 111,113
Water Gallery .................... 71
Watercraft Ltd ............. 72,*78*
Watford Family ................. 52
Welsh National Eisteddfod
  ......................................*126*
Westcott (Karno), Fred
  ....................*68*,72,79 et seq
Whatford, T. ...................... 58
White, Mr .......................... 21
William IV ....................... 117
Witon, Robb ...................... 79
Winchilsea, Earl of .......... 110
Womens Political and Social
  Union ........................... 126
Wren's Island .................... 35
Wrestler, Mr ...................... 59
Wright, Mr ........................ 65
Wyford ............................. 57
Zoffany ........................... 111

ENDPAPERS: The Thames from Molesey Lock to Hampton Reach, showing Ash Island, Tagg's Island with bridge, with Garrick's House, Garrick's Villa and Hampton Church in the background; Hurst Park Racecourse is on the left, with the Cricket Club next door, then Molesey Boat Club, with Tom Tagg's Boat Clubhouse.

# Supporters of the Third Impression

## *Presentation Copies*

**Mrs Gwen Baker**
**Mr Steve Baker**
**Mr David Davis, Chairman, Surrey County Council**
**Cllr Vic Eldridge, Mayor of Elmbridge Borough Council**
**Cllr Mrs Rosemary Dane, Deputy Mayor of Elmbridge Borough Council**
**Mr Leslie Butler, President, Molesey Residents Association**

| | | |
|---|---|---|
| Tony Alderton | Mrs Jane Evans | John Myers |
| Dee Aldridge | Lilian Farwell | D. Partridge |
| Ann Alexander | Daphne Featherstone | Jenni Phillips |
| Dennis & Rita Ashbourne | Caroline Foster | Terry Quinn |
| Mr & Mrs G.Barber | Ian Franklin | Peter Randall |
| Penny Beckett | Steve Goodwin | Mr Reddick |
| Vicky Bevan | Sally Grimstone | Jane Sachdev |
| Mrs Blyther | Lilian Haines | Jean Sanders |
| Russell Brittle | Sue Halliday | Margaret Scott |
| Mrs Browne | Paul Hancock | Patricia Start |
| Stella Burgess | Hazel Hargreaves | Wendy Stevens |
| Joyce Casterton | Wendy Hardy | Anne & Al Stevens |
| Delia Cashman | Iris Hawkes | Caroline Taylor |
| Sue Chaplin | Raymond Hide | Helen Theophanous |
| Ray Cheeseman | Peter Hill | Peter Thomas |
| K.Climpson | Mr Millea | G.D. Tremain |
| Mrs Helena Constable | Mrs L. Hunt | Kate E. Turnbull |
| Sue Coulter | Gill Hurle | Dr. Stephen Twigge |
| Roger Creber | Mrs J. Kirkman | Christine Harrison. |
| Lilian Davenport | Grahame Klipper | Pauline Vandenberghe |
| Annette Davies | David Lanaway | Gill Viner |
| J. Denovan-Smith | Mr & Mrs Leevelock | Bill Waller |
| Mr Dunne | Mr & Mrs Lewington | Elsie Walton |
| Geraldine Eden-Badger | Mrs P.Livingstone | Jane Whishaw |
| Mr & Mrs Edwards | Mrs Lucas | G. Willis |
| Mr M.D. Einchcomb | Roger Marlow | Lia Wright |
| Diana Elder | Mrs J. McGillan | |
| Anne Ephgrave | Karen McLaughlin | *Remaining names unlisted* |